PRAISE for

BUILDING AN AMAZING CAREER AND JODENE HAGER

"Dene impresses me, so I want to be where she is stirring up some good energy."

— Diana Thompson, LMP

"Dene never ceases to amaze me with the array of brilliant ideas that pass through her mind. She has a focus and a commitment to helping people move forward in their lives, be it health, career, or personal growth. And she's funny."

— Janis Lynne, LMP

"Jodene's book is a compelling and interesting read with a good dose of humor. It pulls you along with a variety of quick paced stories, examples, and conclusions. I include her as a key part of my self-care team because her bodywork is some of the most effective I've received."

— Cori Kruger, LMP

"When I was first hired at WellnessOne, Jodene Hager was manager of the Massage department. During that period, our massage department was the most successful it had ever been. Jodene is the only person I know who can do just about any job and do it better than most."

> — Joleen Black, LMP, reported to Jodene at WellnessOne™ of Bellevue

"Dene worked in my office for several years as the Department Team Leader for our Massage Department. I was very impressed with her skills and abilities. She established the basis for my massage team, set in place many policies and standards, made recommendations, and implemented many streamlining and efficiency procedures…still in place today. She is dependable, honest, and a caring individual."

> — Dr. Steven Thain, DC, Owner, WellnessOne of Bellevue ™

"Dene is great! A real leader. Organized. Approachable and warm. A pleasure to be around. I look forward to seeing Dene in particular at our Meetup groups."

> — Alison Butler, LMP, CEO, The Massage Team

"Two words…Talented and Experienced = Jodene Hager of NW Pain Relief. Some people were just born to do certain things and Jodene was born to do massage! As a massage therapist myself, I am picky about who works on me, so if I am wowed by her, you KNOW you will be!"

> — Karen Floyd, PowerTalkLive.com

"Dene could always be counted on to come up with new innovative solutions, follow them through until completion, and always do so with a big smile on her face. I recommend her highly."

> — Dr. Stefan Black, DC

BUILDING AN AMAZING CAREER

Lessons Learned and Marketing Strategies for Health Professionals

HCPRN.org
Health Care Professionals Referral Networking

JODENE "DENE" HAGER, LMP

Book One in the Building an Amazing Career Series

Building an Amazing Career
Lessons Learned and Marketing Strategies for Health Professionals

Copyright ©2011 by Jodene "Dene" Hager, LMP

All rights reserved. No part of this book may be reproduced, transmitted or stored in any form whatsoever without written permission from the author.

Please address all inquiries to:

Jodene "Dene" Hager, LMP
Office (888) 823-7381
www.hcprn.org
www.BuildingAnAmazingCareer.com

Library of Congress Control Number: 2011908151

ISBN: 978-1-935586-34-0

Edited by: Tyler Tichelaar

Cover Design: Maureen Blomgren

Interior Layout: Fusion Creative Works, www.fusioncw.com

For more information please visit: www.BuildingAnAmazingCareer.com

DEDICATION

In memory of my mentor and teacher, Zdenka Daucik, LMP. Your courage to be an innovator will always inspire me. I hope to channel that courage for the days ahead.

To my life partner, my rock, Barbara "Bobbi" Tidwell—who always lifts me up when I'm down, tells me I can do anything I put my mind to, and supports me in every possible way she can. With all my heart, I appreciate you.

To Mom and Dad, I love you no matter what. Without you, I wouldn't be me, and I am grateful to you for that.

To my first term massage instructor who has now been my mentor for a long time, Janis Lynne, LMP. You'll never know just how much of an impact you've had on me. Thank you for lighting the fire under me to get this done.

To all my health care professional friends who just aren't busy enough, I hope this book can turn on some lights for you and help you find a way to change that situation so you will have a longer, more satisfying career.

To all the health care professionals across the nation who so graciously offered their experiences for this book, I give you my humble thanks. May the gift of your lessons learned save many others time, expense, and hardships.

To all the students I've met and haven't yet met, here are all the things I wish I could have told you, wrapped up in a neatly edited package. I can't wait to hear all about your amazing careers.

ACKNOWLEDGMENTS

I want to recognize the following people—my network, my teachers, my mentors, and my friends—for their support, excitement, and belief in me as I followed my ever so mysterious destiny. A huge thank you goes to each of them for always knowing that no matter how much I might meander, I would always come out on top, and reminding me of it when I needed.

Barbara "Bobbi" Tidwell
Misty Nault, MSA, L.Ac.
Cori Kruger, LMP
Zdenka Daucik, LMP
Janis Lynne, LMP
Pam Foster, LMP
Dr. Stefan Black, DC
Joleen Black, LMP
Ruth Werner, LMP, NCBTMB
Marie Maguire, MA, BHE, CMS, CHt, FIBH
Mary Aske
Angela Guest, RN

Jennifer Sheldon, LMP
Salena Rushton
Gene Hamilton
Maureen Blomgren
Deb Blaha, Naturopathic Physician
Shuna Morelli, LMP
Chris Morton, MD
Rebecca Holverstott, LMP
Scott Wilson, LMP
Professor Cathy McDonald
Patrick Snow

CONTENTS

Introduction	13
Part 1: Start Off on the Right Foot	**21**
Chapter 1: Learn to Ask for Help	23
Question Your Assumptions	23
Set Your Frame of Mind	26
Know Your Strengths and Weaknesses	27
Even With a Degree—You Need Help	29
Chapter 2: Pursuing Dreams	33
Visualization of Your Ideal Future	33
Set Your Goals	35
Accept Accountability	38
Chapter 3: Picking a Mentor	39
Exaggerators vs. Real Successful People	39
Mentors Who Share Mistakes	42
What Makes a Great Mentor?	43
Chapter 4: Picking a Coach	45
Why You Should Get a Coach	45
Interviewing Your Coach	47
Hiring Your Coach	53
Chapter 5: Constant Improvement	57
Update Your Training	57
Be Award-Winning	59
Measure Your Success	60
Part 2: Preventing Burnout—Have Work-Life Balance	**65**
Chapter 6: Understanding Your Limitations	67
Be Realistic	67
Introverts—Highly Sensitive People	68
Structure Your Hours—Time Management	71
Getting Help	74
Chapter 7: Self-Care	79
Trading Your Way to a Healthier You	80
Planning for Time Off	83
Chapter 8: Dealing with Adversity	87
Just Not Busy Enough	87

A Deal with the Devil: Insurance Companies	88
Tough Financial Times	90
Support Groups Work Wonders	91
Appreciating What You Have	93
Chapter 9: Dealing with Injuries	97
When I Hurt Myself	97
Chapter 10: Communicating Needs	105
The Big Project Talk	105
Convey Expectations Clearly	107
Learn to Control Your Temper	109

Part 3: Marketing Yourself — **111**

Chapter 11: Your Image	113
You Must Have a Business Card	113
Elevator Speech (30 Second Intro)	115
Focus Your Intentions—Create a Mission Statement	116
Becoming a Specialist	118
Chapter 12: Looking for a Place to Practice	121
Weighing the Pros and Cons of Types of Practice Structures	121
Interviewing for a Space or Position	123
Get It in Writing	133
Working at Home	134
Being Picky is Smart	135
Chapter 13: Selecting a Group Practice	139
Looking to Rent a Group Space	139
Set Expectations in Groups	142
Check out the Clientele	143
Chapter 14: The Offer	145
Don't Jump On It	145
Examine Your Offer	147
Low Paying Jobs	148
Leave on a Positive Note	151
Chapter 15: Everybody's an Entrepreneur	155
Promote the Brand that is YOU	155
Going Out On Your Own	157

Part 4: Networking Like You Mean It — **161**

Chapter 16: Why I Don't Advertise	163
Word-of-Mouth	163

Pros and Cons of Types of Advertising	172
Serve the Greater Good	177
Chapter 17: Building Relationships	181
Being Approachable	181
Following Through	184
Respectfulness and Burning Bridges	185
Chapter 18: Collaboration not Competition	191
Nobody Succeeds Completely Alone	191
They Aren't Your Competition	193
Building Partnerships	194
Interviewing a Potential Partner—Trust Your Gut	196
Healing Gifts vs. Business Minds	198
The "What's In It for Them?" Rule	199
Partnering to Promote Each Other	204
Chapter 19: Networking Groups	207
Networking Is Good For You!	207
Networking Does Not Mean Selling	208
Networking No-No's	209
Master Networker Behaviors	211
Get the Conversation Going	212
Leads Groups	213
Power Referral Partners	217
Chapter 20: Becoming a Leader	221
Get Involved With a Peer Support Group	221
Defer to Others' Expertise	223
Become a Mentor	227
Become an Expert	228
Write a Book, Become a Teacher	229
Bibliography	233
Building an Amazing Career Challenge	239
Building Amazing Partnerships Challenge	241
About Health Care Professionals Referral Networking	245
About Northwest LMP Support Group	247
About the Author	249
Attend a Seminar by Dene	251
Visit Our Website	253

*Success is social:
all the ingredients of success that we
customarily think of as individual—
talent, intelligence, education, effort,
and luck—are intertwined with networks.*

— Wayne Baker, *Achieving Success
Through Social Capital*

INTRODUCTION

In school, the future was looking so bright. The doors would swing open, the clients would come running, and I would finally reach a stage of having enough in my life. My teachers had said something about how important networking was, but I didn't quite get what that really meant. I couldn't wait to graduate and get my license to practice.

From all the books I had read, it seemed so easy to build a practice. Every success formula seemed like it would work for me. From what I had read, I'd make a bunch of money, live comfortably, and help lots of people along the way. I'd print up a bunch of coupons on Valentine's Day, say "Hi" to my neighboring chiropractor, and wham, I'd be busy. I had read all those books about building a successful practice by following formula A, B, and C, and you're done. It was going to be a piece of cake.

Then I was out of school and looking for a job. No one would hire me because I was new and appeared to be almost exactly the same as everyone else applying for a job. It seemed nobody was looking for someone like me because there were just so many of me already out there. There weren't a whole lot of places interested in taking on a newbie. My resume was unimpressive to potential employers because I looked like everyone else fresh out of school who applied.

So I decided to go out on my own and become a sole practitioner with a whopping $1,000 for start-up money. I found an extremely reasonable rental in the closet of a chiropractor's office on a busy street in an affluent city. I couldn't walk around the table completely, but it was so cheap I took it. Seems perfect for someone just starting out, right?

I mailed off hundreds of requests to other practitioners to meet and get to know them. I visited local real estate offices and gave coupons to their agents to give to their clients. I volunteered to give chair massage everywhere I could. I even hired other therapists to help me at some paid chair massage events.

I felt like I had worked my tail off to get people in my office. But then the chiropractor from whom I rented, and who spent most of his time at the local YMCA networking with his basketball buddies, was angry with me for not sending every patient I saw his way. He took me aside to tell me I needed to refer more patients to him.

Even though my schedule was full, the lion's share of it was full of discounted sessions and free demos, and I rarely collected a full session price. Most of that first year, I was barely making enough to keep going. It was a humbling experience to realize that all those formulas I had read about were not actually going to work when I put them into play. It was disappointing to realize that the school admissions rep clearly overstated my income possibilities for my first year. It was infuriating that the chiropractor I worked with wasn't referring clients to me when he wanted me to refer mine to him. I was mad at the world.

Then the worst happened. Within a year after I started out, the chiropractor I subleased from could no longer pay his rent. He closed his doors, giving me little notice, and I had to move my practice out. All the stationery, business cards, advertising, and the work I had put into making my space perfect went down the drain. I had to start from scratch when I was just getting going. The right thing to do was to go get a paying job and build up enough money to move my practice to a new location.

So I quickly found a job in the torture chamber, a cell phone call center, to make ends meet. That quickly drove me completely nuts because I was living away from my life's purpose. I decided I'd try to find another employer since I could not afford to restart my business all over again at a new location. I found a chiropractor willing to pay me as an employee and take me on with my slightly over one year of experience. The office was only a couple of miles down the road from my last one, so I thought it was perfect, and I felt so confident all those clients would follow me.

Then I found out something I really wished I hadn't. When you leave a location and move, you can lose a lot of your clients. It was terrible, especially since after sending my clients a letter so they would know where I had moved, none of them came to see me at my new location. Maybe they wouldn't come merely because their coupons had run out or wouldn't be valid at the new location. Maybe they wouldn't come because they didn't like the place I had moved into. Maybe they just wanted that one freebie massage I had given them. Whatever their reasons were, it seemed I had lost all that work I had put into my first practice simply by moving down the street and taking a short break.

I was angry. I was afraid for my future because the new place wasn't as busy as I had hoped. I had thought that when I worked for someone else, the schedule would just be filled up for me. I wanted to walk in that door with a full schedule, but it wasn't full. How was I going to get this new chiropractor to send me more patients?

Not three months later, the massage manager who had hired me moved on to another job. It seemed like terrible timing. Feeling sort of rudderless after that manager left, I did what I always like to do when I'm feeling out of alignment—I got a chiropractic adjustment from the clinic's owner. Then he offered me the job of manager for the massage practice at two clinics. Strained for cash and hungry for opportunity, I took the job.

He set me up with an incentive plan. The busier I made the clinic, the better off I'd be. The only thing was that I would have to make all those therapists be busy. I'd have to teach other therapists how to create their practices there when I was still figuring it out myself.

We started with me at one clinic and two other therapists at the other clinic. It seemed like it would be easy enough to manage. But once I was put in charge, I realized that one of the two therapists had one foot out the door, and the other therapist was getting ready to leave the practice and take over half its massage patients with her. The chiropractors and the massage therapists weren't on the same team and weren't working together. I felt like I had just been made the captain of a sinking ship.

By very selectively hiring people with a team mentality, mentoring them one by one, and a lot of trial and error, I made a new success formula. The underlying formula was simple—network with each other, teach each other what we do best, create team goals, and hold everyone accountable for his or her own success by having established goals. The therapists learned how to get referrals from the chiropractors, and the massage therapists learned how to refer clients to the chiropractors. Both practices grew rapidly. One year later, we had grown into a team of twelve massage therapists. There were no "short" forty-hour workweeks. Keeping up with the growing pace of the business took a lot of effort, but the friendships I created at that office remain some of my best relationships to this day.

The health care world at large can benefit from having the formula I learned applied to it: By networking with each other, sharing our strengths, pooling our capabilities, and working together, we can build practices faster and stronger than anyone would ever think possible. More importantly, we can help our patients better by creating a "climate of helpfulness" in our integrative medicine community.

This book is written for health care practitioners who want something better out of their careers, not the people who work in their careers because it's a job. My advice is for those healers who want to change the world with what they do and be the best possible health care practitioners they can be. I wrote this book for you—I hope that a stroke of my pen can save you hours of agony in your career.

This book is meant to take you from start to finish in your career. The first section, "Start Off on the Right Foot," will give you a foundation of thoughts upon which to start your career. The second section, "Preventing Burnout—Have Work-Life Balance," offers thoughts on how to keep your career longer by preventing the symptoms associated with burnout. The third section, "Marketing Yourself," talks about a lot of things I didn't learn in school that I really wish I had been told about practicing in the real world. The fourth section, "Networking Like You Mean It," will give you thoughts on how to become a master networker and a leader in your community during your career.

At the end of the book, I will ask you to submit lessons you learned in the field that you wished you had learned in school with the "Building an Amazing Career Challenge" and the "Building Amazing Partnerships Challenge." Get some free publicity and help other health care professionals avoid the same problems you've faced.

I challenge you to learn as much as you can about what your health care practitioner neighbor does. I challenge you to step outside of your practice walls and look beyond your differences in approach. Find your strengths and pool your abilities to help people. Together, you and your neighbors can become a force of nature that will empower your mutual success.

> *And the stories that you'll find here reveal something that is extremely simple but awe-inspiringly powerful—that people want to do the right thing, they want to create and offer quality things, they want to do good in the world, and if you give them the opportunity and the resources to do so, they will shine. Here's to all the stories that are yet to be told.*
> — Jim Alling, COO T-Mobile

Part 1

START OFF ON THE RIGHT FOOT

Chapter 1

LEARN TO ASK FOR HELP

Chapter Summary: When we get out of school, our heads are full of inspiration and ideas on how we're going to become successful. Some of us don't know where to start, while others seem to figure out these things naturally. We need to learn to call on all our resources and ask for help when we don't know the answers in order to start off our careers right.

QUESTION YOUR ASSUMPTIONS

I've often volunteered to speak at schools on practitioner panels or as a solo guest speaker. My teachers from years past will contact me and ask me to share with their classes my experiences in the field to give their students advice on business, a healthy reality check, or just to dispel myths. Speaking to future health practitioners is something I love to do because I want to save everyone time by teaching others not to duplicate the mistakes I made or observed along the way.

One panel I served on required the students to interview the panelists. My friend, Pam Foster, LMP, was leading this class. She brought to me a student who thought he had it all figured out, although he was receptive to listening to my thoughts. I could tell he felt he had it all figured out by his disposition. He said he'd like to be an evidence-based massage therapist. I suggested that he get involved in research and learn what evidence we have now. If he wanted to be an evidence-based practitioner, he needed to be more than just familiar with research studies; he would need to be able to answer questions about them.

In the process of our conversation, we learned that he didn't want to work with someone who practiced energy work, but to work for a local chiropractor. I cautioned him that very often chiropractors might refer to energy while others might be evidence-based only and staunchly against referring to energy in their practices. While energy work may not be real to him, energy work can be very real to patients who have not found solutions to their problems in any other way. After explaining this to him, I suggested he consider employment with a physical therapist, where it was less likely that any reference to energy would take place. The lesson here was that he needed to examine his assumptions further before he decided he would be a perfect fit for working with just any chiropractor. I've heard that over two hundred types of chiropractic modalities exist—it's important not to lump every practitioner into one category since all of us have diverse gifts and training, and diverse methods for applying those gifts and training.

> *Story Time:*
>
> *There was an "A" student I knew who had graduated from massage school as the valedictorian of her class. Everyone thought she was going to be wildly successful as a therapist. She had a part-time job as a waitress and a great low-budget set-up for her business. Unfortunately, all her advertising didn't do enough to keep*

> her in business, and she didn't last long in the profession. Just because people get good grades in school does not mean they know how to run a business or grow one.

He who is ashamed of asking is ashamed of learning.
— Danish Proverb

First of all, recognize that you need to find out so much more information about the work you're about to do if you are just starting out. If you're already working in the field, you can probably still take away some interesting information from this book. Listen to all the available people around you who have been successful and hear their stories. Remember, they may be leaving out important details about how the process works, and those details will be yours to discover on your own.

There is a common myth that asking for help displays that you are weak in a certain area—whichever area you're asking about. When we ask for help, we often fear we will look like fools, or we will be laughed at, or worse. The truth is that asking for help communicates to others that we may not have all the answers to the questions out there, but we are willing to use our resources to find them.

Many people think that really successful people never need to ask for help. Nothing could be farther from the truth; in fact, many successful people say it is important to know well your own strengths and weaknesses, it is wise to learn how to refer to someone else's expertise, and a true skill is learning to delegate tasks to others who are better skilled than you in a certain area. Highly successful corporations use this model all the time by hiring consultants to come in to fill in the gaps in their skills—no one can be all things to all people.

SET YOUR FRAME OF MIND

In one of my favorite books, *The 7 Habits of Highly Effective People*, author Stephen Covey discusses key habits that will make your application of my book more successful. These key habits are the same ones you need to practice in your everyday career. I recommend you read Covey's book or listen to the audio version right away if you haven't already.

You will find that many of these high level views of what it takes to be a highly effective person cross over to what is needed for success in the health care profession. To be successful in health care, it takes a proactive, goal-oriented individual, one who can set priorities to create partnerships based on mutual respect, and one who can find the right partners who will continuously work to improve their skills as healers in their given specialties. You must first learn to be proactive about your career. Don't let your career happen to you; make sure you happen to your career.

In his book, Covey also talks about stages of dependence, independence, and interdependence. Once we realize which stage we are in, we can focus our efforts upon moving forward in that stage and the next one. If you are a person who feels comfortable working in an employer/employee relationship, you are most likely in the stage of dependence. If you are a person who is wishing to move on and do your own thing, you're most likely moving from a stage of dependence into independence. But it is the third stage—interdependence with others—that I invite you to strive for and to learn the most about during your health care career, whether you're an employee in a large group practice or a sole practitioner. When you call upon the strengths of others, you magnify your possibilities for yourself and your patients. In this particular mindset, you can create new possibilities.

KNOW YOUR STRENGTHS AND WEAKNESSES

Were you once an administrative assistant? Were you possibly a business consultant in your past? Did you coordinate lots of projects in your previous work? Or perhaps you have no work experience at all. A very efficient way to figure out your strengths is to visit www.StrengthsFinder.com and take the online assessment produced by Gallup and created by Donald O. Clifton, Ph.D. It will give you an idea of your abilities more clearly than you can imagine.

A fault is fostered by concealment.
— Virgil

It's important when starting a career to know your strengths—and your weaknesses. This knowledge can give you some insight about why some things come to you naturally compared to other things that seem to take all of your energy to accomplish. When you identify your strengths, you can quickly see those areas where you will need help. Once you know what you will need help to do, delegate those tasks to someone else who has the strengths or skills needed, or accept some advice from the experienced. If you work for someone else, you may find that many tasks have been taken off your plate. That situation doesn't mean you shouldn't take time to look at your abilities and evaluate yourself. Look to others who are good at what they do to fill in your blanks. Draw on their experiences to enhance your own abilities.

If your past has proven that you tend to be a depressed or anxious person, then you are much more likely to be unhappy with your current situation, no matter how good or bad it might be. It will be a struggle to change your mindset when things are going badly at your office. You may begin to complain to others whom you feel you can confide in, but then you have become a liability to the company and present a problem to the business. Take care of any mood issues first before trying to start a business.

> *Story Time:*
>
> *A practitioner I know has a horrible reputation for being a very negative person with an overbearing personality. He won't accept coaching, hates every job he's ever had, blames the world for his failures, doesn't take responsibility for any of his mistakes, and discounts good advice from those around him—and he is well known for it. This particular person has asked me for a job in the past, and I have had to let him know, politely and respectfully, that I'm not hiring, simply based on the fact that at the time I wasn't hiring, but even so, I wouldn't have hired him because I had heard he'd caused problems at other practices by gossiping with other team members about policies he disagreed with. Even if he might have actually worked well with me and I could help him to turn his bad habits around, I didn't see the value in taking on someone who might be really time-intensive to help. This person unfortunately continues to have a hard time finding a job because of his reputation and bad recommendations. Sadly, he created these problems for himself and may never understand what he's done wrong that makes other people unwilling to work with him.*

What could this person do to turn around these bad habits? First, he should learn to ask for help. He should learn to listen to people who have been successful, and he should consider finding a coach just to get him out of bad habits—even if he's going to be an employee. Coaches aren't just for business owners—they can be for employees who have changes they need to make to their habits. An Image Coach, a Life Coach, or a Career Coach are some options. The first step to improving a situation is to be willing to notice your own weaknesses and acknowledge them as weaknesses, then ask for help. When a situation has gone badly, one should be able to look back in hindsight and gather the lessons learned from that situation. If a person can't find the lessons learned, then he should solicit someone else to help him change his perspective and learn how to confront his own weaknesses.

EVEN WITH A DEGREE—YOU NEED HELP

> *Empty pockets never held anyone back.*
> *Only empty heads and empty hearts can do that.*
> — Norman Vincent Peale

Growing up, my family didn't have a lot of things I saw other families around me possessing. It was expected that we were not going to go to college unless we found a way to pay for it ourselves. Through practical experience, I have learned that people with lots of degrees even have trouble running their own businesses or practices. Having a degree does not mean you have all the skills you need to be successful as a business owner. This skill only comes with practical experience and a lot of trial and error.

> *Residency programs will continue to offer the bare nuts and bolts of practicing medicine but they have never discussed the true practice of medicine…and that is bad business.*
> — Gregory A. Buford, MD FACS and
> Steven E. House, *Beauty and the Business: Practice, Profits, and Productivity, Performance and Profitability*

In writing this book, I interviewed many people in the health care professions to understand better their experiences, gain from their knowledge, and to find out what information they wish had been given to them at the start of their careers. Maureen Daniek MSW, a Life Transition Coach specializing in working with individuals who are experiencing major life changes, says of her education:

> I went through undergrad and graduate training and never had a single class offered that focused on the idea of building a practice. There was an assumption that if you had an advanced degree and you were good, it would just happen on its own—magically. I think also that when I was in grad school there was a bias against thinking like a "business person" because they are all greedy and as healers we are a cut above. I hope there is more awareness today in the healing field educational programs—that folks need some assistance with tools required in the building of a practice.

> *Drop the idea that you need to get a degree in order to be successful.… The degree doesn't matter as much as being up-to-date with the latest developments in your field or profession.*
> — Anna Wildermuth, author of *Change One Thing: Discover What's Holding You Back—and Fix it—With the Secrets of a Top Executive Image Consultant*

Some of us in the medical field do not have our advanced education degrees. Maybe it is because circumstances haven't given us the chance to go back to school. Whatever our reasons, some of the most successful people I know were not "A" students or do not have business degrees.

KEY LESSONS:

- Question the assumptions you made about how the "real world" would be when you left school.

- Know your strengths and your weaknesses—ask for help from your peers, use your resources, and use your network.

- You don't need a degree to be successful in business.

Chapter 2

PURSUING DREAMS

Chapter Summary: You have to get a picture of your future in your head that is so vivid you can feel it with all your senses. Get your mind frame set for success and set your goals in a practical way you can use to hold yourself accountable against them.

VISUALIZATION OF YOUR IDEAL FUTURE

Plenty of books, videos, seminars, and coaches can help you to find the visualization technique that works best for you. Many techniques revolve around using meditation and relaxation for healing—it's very important when you're a healer to stay grounded. The fantastic thing about visualization is that it can be applied anywhere in your life and not just in building your future.

If you want to make good things happen in your life, think in terms of wishes instead of goals.
— Keith Ellis, *The Magic Lamp: Goal Setting for People Who Hate Setting Goals*

First find a place where you can relax quietly. It may not necessarily be at your house. Possibly, a quiet park, or my personal favorite, a secluded spot on the beach, will work. If you cannot leave your home, make sure you let your friends and family know you need a moment of peace so you can accomplish this task. When you're getting started, peace and quiet are essential for learning how to calm your spirit so you can really listen to yourself thoroughly. It's best to start every day by doing this exercise.

Here is one technique that may work for you:

1. Write down your goals and dreams and lay them on a sheet in front of you.

2. Find a quiet place to take a long series of deep breaths. Quiet your mind and soften your eyes. When thoughts come along, quickly push them away and draw your attention back to your breathing.

3. Think of how it feels to have accomplished the goals on the sheet of paper in front of you. How does it taste to be successful? How does it smell? What emotions come to you? What do you look like as a successful person?

Deb Blaha, naturopathic physician, successfully uses visualization in her practice. "When I want to get busier, I think about the people I want to see. I write down their names in my scheduler or I flip through old charts."

I have no right to work on the 'how' until I can taste, touch, smell, feel, hear, emotionalize, and 'own the vision.' The vision comes first and then I see 'how' to accomplish my dreams.
— Larry Olsen, *Get a Vision and Live It*

> Story Time:
>
> One clinic I worked with would have a huddle every day before starting to see patients. They would put a written goal on the

> *printed calendar of patients for the day where everyone could see them. They aimed as a team for new patients and total visits for that day. While it may seem that this exercise is all about creating numbers, it is essential to have partly a business mind when you're running a practice, and you must move past any thoughts that you can't think about the numbers.*

Anybody can dream up goals to pursue, but most of us never achieve them. The reason why is because we lack an understanding of where to start or how to execute them. A great formula for executing your goals is:

1. First, remember that you must focus on what is most important of all to your office—productivity. You're business is not going to stay open if you're not productive. If you're an employee, you're not going to keep a job if you're not productive.

2. Have a place where the goal is written down and verbalized so everyone can see it and hear it.

3. Measure how well you did against the goals at the end of the day or the next morning. Get fired up if you all did well toward reaching your goal—celebrate the achievement of getting it right.

4. Hold everyone accountable in the group for the practice goals, and coach people when they are having trouble following through on their roles.

SET YOUR GOALS

Over the years, I have stumbled on many opportunities. One time when I was dealing with an injured shoulder and wrist, I went back to the corporate world of project management and business analysis and had the opportunity to consult at such companies as Microsoft, Intel, T-Mobile, and BP. I learned a lot while I was there by hanging out with some seriously smart people. How did I get those jobs without a degree? I feel it had a lot to do with knowing the right people, being willing to take risks, being available for the opportunity, selling what skills I did have, and sometimes working myself to the bone.

During these experiences, I researched much about goal setting, measuring success, and executing your goals. These projects showed me over and over again a concept that Shuna Morelli, LMP described well. She explained to me that she thinks of goal setting as being similar to when you're skiing down a hill; don't look all the way down the hill—just focus on the three feet in front of you. What she was trying to convey was to slow down your approach and just take it day-by-day—don't let it overwhelm you because, whatever your goal, it can be achieved.

You don't have to hire a consultant to help you set your goals. In fact, it is much better to take a template and write down your personal goals for your work instead of having someone else do it for you. When I worked as a consultant, I quickly realized that consultants don't know everything—they just know how to find information on anything. Google and other web search engines are consultants' best friends; as a consultant, I knew how to use them effectively, and I used them very often to answer questions the client had asked me. I like to call it "Googling for Dollars" since what the client then was paying for was information and not experience. If you hire anyone to provide consulting for you, pay for experience, not information you can fetch yourself if you have the time.

Start with listening to your passion—what gets you fired up the most. Most often, your passion can also be interpreted as your purpose. Contrary to many schools of thought, your purpose in life may not always remain the same and can shift with new experiences and inspiration. Choose your personal passion that you know you will be the best at, and that will bring others significant value, and you will probably find your calling. By doing so, I came as close to finding my life's purpose as I've ever been.

Let's imagine that your life is exactly the way you want it to be. Write down all your achievements thus far in every manner possible. Next, rank each small detailed part of this imagined reality by priority to you—be sure to place the most important as the highest, and do not be distracted by supporting goals; they can't all be first. For each goal, set a timeframe for its accomplishment—six months, one year, two years, five years, etc. Revisit these goals and your plan frequently. Keep yourself focused on what you need to do next to keep moving toward those goals. As you learn as you go, revise as necessary those goals and the steps to reach them.

One method I have used to keep myself focused is a dream board. My dream was to have certain things in my life like more travel, more health, and more abundance. I created my dream board by going through a bunch of magazines and clipped photos and pasting them on a large sheet of construction paper. I had sailboats, far away tropical places, and a hand holding money as if it were going to hand it to me (because at the time I was completely broke!). These were the most compelling images to me. I posted this dream board in my kitchen where I would see it every time I went to check the fridge for a bite to eat. It helped me to focus my intentions, and it helped me to get through tough times in my life when I was heavily distracted by the normal day-to-day activities of life.

ACCEPT ACCOUNTABILITY

If you want to be successful, you have to take 100 percent responsibility of everything you experience in your life.
— Jack Canfield and Janet Switzer, *The Success Principles: How to Get from Where You Are to Where You Want to Be*

The economy is down; should you blame the economy? Your clients just dropped off the radar; should you blame it on the weather? No. Take it as a cue that you missed a step somewhere, and be accountable that you may have missed something recently in your work. Maybe you got too caught up with treating the patients you had for awhile so you didn't market yourself; now, you're subsequently slow. The bottom line is that you must hold yourself accountable for your own success and learn from your mistakes as much as you can.

Sometimes business outcomes hurt, but re-framing helps us to accept whatever happens by looking for the silver lining and the lessons to be learned.
— David Ryback, Jim Cathcart, and David Nour, *ConnectAbility: 8 Keys to Building Stronger Partnerships with Your Colleagues and Your Customers*

KEY LESSONS:

- Visualize your goals
- Set your mind frame for success
- Write down your goals in a place you will see them
- Own your mistakes and learn from them.
- Consultants don't know everything. A little research on your own goes a long way.

Chapter 3

PICKING A MENTOR

Chapter Summary: We learn through having successes and making mistakes. Our subconscious categorizes these experiences as positive and negative reinforcements. We learn through watching others and hearing their stories.

EXAGGERATORS VS. REAL SUCCESSFUL PEOPLE

Believe nothing, no matter where you read it, or who said it, no matter if I have said it, unless it agrees with your own reason and your own common sense.
— Buddha

Don't always think you have to pick the most successful person to be your mentor. While it is enormously helpful to find that person, some people may have trouble conveying the truth about where they are at in their business. Most people want to project very successful images even though they may be struggling financially. Other people may see themselves as successful but not be of the same caliber as what you consider to be successful. For example, one person may be perfectly happy to make $30,000 a year and only see a select number of patients every week while another person won't consider himself successful until he breaks

$100,000 per year. I have met several practitioners over the years who have faked their success to their own detriment. In some areas, for sure, the phrase "fake it 'til you make it" just does not apply.

> *Story Time:*
>
> *One doctor I knew had received an award for being one of the nation's top doctors and proudly displayed the award in his lobby for all his patients, colleagues, and employees to see. One day, I learned that he had paid for the trophy from an advertising firm who puts together a directory. The very clever advertising firm does outreach to established doctors in the area and creates a trophy for them to show their position in their field—at a high price. First, the advertising firm is deceiving the doctor into thinking he actually won something. While it's the doctor's duty to be honest with his accomplishments, some people would see right through this advertisement method; others will really think they have won something even though they had to pay for it, but others will go along with receiving the award, knowing a falsehood is taking place. Realize that some awards may be paid for and are not always given out of respect for accomplishments.*

Some businesspeople may claim they can earn three times the average annual income for their occupation, and they will advertise their incredible success to their communities. What they often don't include in that information is that figure is a gross income figure based on best-case scenarios—they don't take into consideration all the expenses that go into running a practice or all the things that tend to go wrong. What they also don't include is how long it took to build the business up to that level and that it's not likely to happen quickly—not the first year, and possibly not the second or even third year—and it all depends on the person and his or her drive to succeed. If you plan on having a really nice looking space, consider all the things it's going to take to make that space look good. If you want to attract high-end clients, you have to remember you must have a high-end appearance for you and your space. It takes time to meet those prospective clients, and your friends and family do not count as starter practice seed—do not count on them to follow through on their promises; many people I know have been horribly disappointed when friends and family don't follow through on their promises to do business with them.

While a successful appearing practitioner might seem like a great potential mentor because he is claiming to be making a decent gross income, he is really promoting an illusion. It is your job to weed that person's illusions out and find the lessons he can actually teach you. Some people find that they must appear successful to be successful, but that is only true to a point. By acting more successful than they really are, they are doing a disservice to those people who desire to learn from them by literally not being honest with what has transpired to get them to where they are, and by not being forthright about where they really are. Consider the possibility that the amazingly successful looking person you just saw may not actually have enough money to pay his office rent next month.

The truth is it is very hard to know how successful someone really is and you should use all your judgment skills to put together an accurate picture. It is immensely difficult to determine the accurate picture unless you have access to all the person's records, which I definitely don't recommend you ask to see. The bottom line is you should take your time to get to know someone to see whether he or she is truly a success. The person with the modest practice might actually be the most successful one around.

MENTORS WHO SHARE MISTAKES

> *My humanity is bound up in yours,*
> *for we can only be human together.*
> — Desmond Tutu

One thing that has held true for me throughout my career is the importance of having a mentor who shares his or her mistakes with you. Learn from such mentors by analyzing their mistakes and thinking of them as mistakes you now don't have to make so you can learn from them; your mentor just saved you a ton of time by your not having to duplicate his problems. I give mentors the respect of listening to their stories to gain value, and I am careful whom I tell about my mentors. You may not want to reveal who is mentoring you because it may associate you with the person, and that may not be what you want in the long run for your career.

Sometimes, it is better not to ask someone to be your mentor. While some people are extremely helpful and giving by nature and will gladly accept that title of respect, others will see your request as a burden upon their time and will not be interested. The reasons why they may not want to be your mentor can be mysterious and personal to them, and they need not be sought out. Instead, simply pick the person's brain in small doses when you see or interact with him. This way, you will acquire a pool of information to build upon and receive knowledge from others' experiences, which could save you a lot of time and money you might otherwise invest to learn the same things.

> *The biggest difference is in the leadership. It was better for us.*
> *We had more coaches and mentors to help us. A lot of the younger*
> *players today suffer from a lack of direction.*
> — Isaiah Thomas

> *Story Time:*
>
> *One of my mentors, who had both mistakes and successes to share with me, once shared that she had accepted much of her work under the table. This particular massage therapist had been in business for many years and had been around the block quite a bit. Her mistake was not paying her taxes to the IRS when she was accepting the income. When the mistake eventually caught up with her, she was given a hefty fine. Now that she is older and trying to retire, it has caught up with her even more because she will have a very small social security check for the rest of her life. We often only think about the short-term punishment for our mistakes if we get caught, and not the things that will affect us for the rest of our lives. But a mistake can often have long-term consequences.*
>
> *This mentor made herself invaluable to me because she was willing to share a very hard lesson learned in a genuine and honest way. She has also been mentoring me since the start of my career, and I plan to keep her around as long as I possibly can.*

WHAT MAKES A GREAT MENTOR?

Sometimes, mentors just happen and there is no formalization of the relationship. Teachers from your school are often great mentors. If you connect with an instructor at school, keep that relationship going because it may be very advantageous over the years. I decided to have multiple mentors to pool information from over a period of time; most of them I've never actually had a formal conversation with about establishing a mentoring relationship. Their experiences changed over the years, they learned more as they went, and I did my best to listen to their ups and downs. It's important to stay in touch and learn with them as they continue to learn. I still have many mentors from my time in school.

> *I was lucky that I met the right mentors
> and teachers at the right moment.*
> — James Levine

Mentors can be for a reason, a season, or a lifetime. If you feel a real connection with someone, no matter how much the person has screwed up, there are lessons to be learned from that person so keep him or her around—even if it needs to be at arm's length. Absorb what lessons you can about your mentors' mistakes and never discount knowing them simply because they made a bunch of mistakes. If someone is flaky, learn from his flakiness and consider him a mentor for a reason. If someone is just passing through on her way to her next adventure, consider her a mentor for a season. If someone is keeping in touch with you, nurturing your relationship, values you, lifts you up, and sets you straight when you need to be, consider that person a mentor for a lifetime.

KEY LESSONS:

- Be skeptical of the "wildly successful"—they may be in debt up to their eyeballs.

- Get to know someone really well and absorb everything you can learn from that person whether or not he or she is successful.

- Mentors may come and go from your life, but whatever you do, you should always have them.

Chapter 4

PICKING A COACH

Chapter Summary: Call them what you want—life coaches, business coaches, consultants, mentors, or advisers—if you are going to start a business, it is important that you consider hiring a business coach. If you're an employee and you're struggling to be successful, consider getting help from a coach as well.

WHY YOU SHOULD GET A COACH

> *A coach is someone who can give correction without causing resentment.*
> — John Wooden

The most successful people I know hire a coach and cite it as the main reason they are successful. As far as I know, nobody has ever been born an all-knowing entrepreneur or fantastic practitioner with all the skills needed to thrive. Sometimes our mentors are unavailable for help on specific topics about starting a business or they cannot be there as often as we may need them.

Here are some of the reasons you should consider having a coach:

1. You're starting a business and don't know where to start.

2. Your career or practice is stalling in growth.

3. You don't have business skills in your experience such as negotiation skills, building a brand, managing people, or salesmanship.

4. You want to move your career to a new level and aren't sure how to go about it.

5. You want to be seen as a leader and need to learn how to present yourself as such and the steps necessary to become one.

6. You need a support network for critical business decision-making and your mentors are too busy to help.

7. You've got lots of fantastic ideas floating around in your head, but you lack the skills to execute them and put them into action.

8. You're burned out and need an influx of new and fresh ideas.

Business coaches can run the gambit on what they can provide for you. Some are industry or task specific. Some are short-term relationships to address a particular project or issue, and others include long on-going agreements to address issues as they arise. A coach is there to help you identify and recognize your strengths and weaknesses, clarify your goals for your future, and create a strategy to execute. The best coach is someone who has actually done the job at hand in his or her prior experience. Unfortunately, a new coach is someone who may not have a lot of business background, so carefully consider the person's experience before hiring him or her as a coach. Choose a coach who is familiar with your industry or particular type of project. Ask the prospective coach for recommendations from other clients.

> *A life coach does for the rest of your life what a personal trainer does for your health and fitness.*
> — Elaine MacDonald

Most great coaches are excellent at helping you to identify limiting beliefs and to get past them in an efficient manner. Coaches are great for having someone to hold you accountable for your productivity until you can make being productive a habit.

Coaches should never give you legal or financial advice unless they are also lawyers or financial advisors. Your coach should not make business decisions for you—you need to make the call whether a decision is feasible. Do not blame a coach for giving you bad advice; you should blame yourself for taking that bad advice without doing more investigating first to determine whether it was bad. Question, question, question before running with an idea.

INTERVIEWING YOUR COACH

Unfortunately, no single fantastic way exists to select a coach. Consider that, similarly, there isn't a single, perfectly proven method to selecting a lifemate. I know a very kind and talented therapist who raved about his coach, but when I visited the therapist's office, I was taken aback by its lack of professionalism. I thought to myself, "Wouldn't his coach have come to his office and told him to stop using that ugly towel by the door to get rid of the draft under the door, or to clean up that mess in the corner, or to decorate the space a little better so it was more welcoming?" It was clear to me that the new coach had provided value by finding ways to get more patients in the door, but it was also apparent to me that the coach hadn't completed the job by providing coaching on making sure the space was welcoming, or by encouraging client retention by creating a professional image.

Interview questions you should consider asking when hiring a coach are:

1. **What is your background?** Look for someone to coach you who has been in your line of work before and can understand where you're coming from when times are hard. At the very least, consider someone who has done something similar in the same industry. The coach should immediately be able to understand the nature of your business without absorbing lots of your valuable paid time while you explain it. You want to get somebody who not only has a lot of experience in business, but who can also come up with fresh, new ideas and innovative approaches for your business.

2. **What are you doing differently now than you were doing five years ago?** If you want to see whether a coach is keeping up-to-date on current trends, such as the latest developments in technology, then you want to know definitively how comfortable this coach is with technology—leaving technology out of your practice will have a lasting negative impact on how successful you could become.

3. **How broad of a client range have you worked with?** Ask for references from those clients because what others say about the coach will tell you a lot about that person. Remember, however, that some people have worked out kickback agreements to help them acquire new clients. They pay for great raving reviews so they can look good to potential new clients. You want to know that your future coach has worked with a broad variety of satisfied clients and not a bunch of friends who will say nice things about him.

4. **What do you consider to be your finest selling point in your coaching?** Ask this question to determine whether the coach is a compassionate person, a direct person, or he or she is about encouragement. A good coach won't just bark orders every time you speak with him. Good coaches are not drill sergeants. They are people with a combination of great people skills, business skills, and sales skills.

5. **How often will you be available to speak between our coaching sessions?** Some coaches will prefer a very structured format for their sessions while others will not mind at all if you call them anytime. This preference is something you should know, and you should choose a coach whose availability will meet your needs. If you have someone who is available all the time, will you be available enough to take advantage of the possible extra cost that goes with that availability? If you need someone you can talk to on holidays or weekends, think to ask that coach how he feels about being contacted during those times. What is his turnaround time on your requests? If you have to wait quite a while to get an answer, perhaps this coach

is too busy or has efficiency issues he needs to resolve for himself. It's always a red flag when someone can't get back to you in a timely manner—move on if the coach seems unorganized or has too many clients already. You want to get your money's worth, and you won't with someone who barely has time for you.

6. **What services will you provide for me as my coach?** Will your coach consult you on your image? Will she tell you what you need to change in your office to be more successful? How will she go about these types of things? Will she take a look at your website for usability? Will she help you to do a market analysis of the area? Will she help you figure out your taxes or point you in the direction of someone who can? You want someone who provides you with unique consulting for your particular situation; not someone who provides you with generalizations and old advice you can easily find by surfing the web.

7. **How big do you think I could grow?** Some coaches reach for the stars while others just aim for the middle ground. Do you want to reach for the stars? Think about how high you want to aim with your career while talking to the prospective coach to see whether he or she has a perspective that matches your goals.

8. **How will you coach me when I'm doing something you disagree with?** If a coach doesn't respect you as an individual and treats you poorly, just remember you are paying that person handsomely to treat you poorly.

9. **How will you communicate with me?** Email, phone, video chat—there are plenty of ways to stay in touch

with a coach, but you must pick the coach who has the best way—and that means the way that works for you. Personally, I love a coach who will let me email him or her anytime I want. I really don't like too many phone calls. Other people may not feel comfortable with email and will want someone who is available by phone anytime.

10. How much does your coaching cost? Do you have a prepay discount available? Is the cost ongoing or do you have a set fee for lifetime coaching? Remember that you will eventually tap out that person's experience, and you shouldn't continue the relationship when you feel there is nothing left to be offered unless it's in the agreement to have lifetime coaching for a set fee. Sometimes it's just good to have a sounding board when you are experienced and doing well.

Try to interview at least five different coaches if not more when you're considering hiring someone, and try to get at least two recommendations for each. Don't stop at the first great person you talk to; otherwise, you may miss out on someone better. If the person cannot provide recommendations, throw that coach out of the stack of candidates immediately. Get an idea for all the services that each one can provide. Look at their successful clients' websites and read the clients' recommendations for the coaches.

Take a moment to ponder whether this person's personality will mesh well with yours. Ask yourself these questions:

1. Would I like to talk to this person on an ongoing basis?
Was it excruciating to complete the interview conversation? Was it awkward and uncomfortable getting him or

her to talk to you? A great coach will be an approachable, confident person with a great sense of humor to lift you up when you need it. He should feel as if he will admit he doesn't have all the answers, but he knows how to find them or to teach you how to find them.

2. **Would I feel comfortable telling this person everything that is going on in my business?** If you're having financial issues, will the coach respect your decision not to take her advice if she asks you to spend money? Will she work within your budget while times are thin? You must feel comfortable talking about your annual salary goals with this person.

3. **How did the prospective coach react when you challenged him or her with the interview questions?** Did he seem defensive or welcoming of them?

4. **Does the coach seem to have a good sense of ethics?** A great coach has no problem telling you the truth when you have a bad idea. She should never ask you to do something that is against your better judgment or is illegal.

5. **Does he do a good job of maintaining his own clients' confidentiality?** When you asked about previous clients, did he give you lots of names, specifics, and problems those people faced? If so, throw that coach out of the list right away. You do not need a coach to air your dirty laundry.

Remember, the coach is also interviewing you to see how much he or she might be able to earn with you, what your expectations are, and if you're a good fit as a client for him or her. Chemistry between you and coach is critical to the success of any coaching relationship.

HIRING YOUR COACH

Before you sign the dotted line, make sure to be clear about what you expect from your coach. Get on paper what is to transpire in the relationship. Get a clear understanding of the services you are going to pay for in the process of having a coach. Do you get one-on-one time, or is it always a group coaching session? Are you able to contact the coach as frequently as you wish without additional fees? Does the coach provide a discounted prepay arrangement for paying up front? Is the person's compensation ongoing or does he have a "coaching for life" package you can buy? I highly suggest you consider a coach who provides a coaching for life package. That way you can get value out of the relationship in an ongoing fashion because there will always come a point when you have tapped out what that person can teach you. Then you move forward on your own or you hire a different coach to take you to the next level. It is immensely important to choose a coach familiar with your industry.

When you're looking for a coach, it's very similar to hiring a financial advisor. Giving clients results usually generates most of their business and the clients tell people about their fantastic results. Word-of-mouth is the best mechanism for finding a coach. Ask your peers or local business association whether they would recommend any coaches, or if not, find out who they know who uses a coach. Then interview the person using the coach to feel out how he is doing to see whether the coach is worth the price. Often, people are snowed into thinking they have gotten a lot of value when they really haven't. Anybody can call him- or herself a coach, so choose wisely before jumping into a potentially expensive agreement.

Be cautious of coaches with lots of letters after their names. Those letters may simply be certifications or association memberships for which they paid handsomely and that really mean nothing in regards to their qualifications. However, all those letters don't by any means suggest that the person may not have the right qualifications.

You can also check out business coach associations, including:

- International Coach Federation: www.coachfederation.com

- International Coaching Council: www.international-coaching-council.com

- Worldwide Association of Business Coaches: www.wabccoaches.com

- European Mentoring & Coaching Council: www.emccouncil.org

When you're weeding out prospects, don't simply use Google to look up a local business coach. You may have to choose a coach who lives far away to get what you need. In such a case, I'd use video to help the coach see your practice location and give you ideas. Use a free video call service to communicate with the coach, or if all else fails, just use the phone. Always ask the coach to view your space and check out what you've already got going on. This review will help the coach to determine whether you are wasting time on a task that will do your business no good, and it can also be an excellent way to save time and money by avoiding the costs associated with meeting face-to-face.

KEY LESSONS:

- You may need a coach if you're self-employed or even an employee.

- Be selective when choosing a coach and interview thoroughly. It can be a large investment.

Chapter 5

CONSTANT IMPROVEMENT

Chapter Summary: It is your duty as a health care professional to work toward a goal of always getting better at what you do. Measure your success and take stock in your accomplishments; just don't spend all day measuring.

UPDATE YOUR TRAINING

There was a time in my life when I was stagnant and I didn't feel like I was growing. One day in the Pike Place Market, I stumbled upon a wonderful small wall hanging. I now have this wonderful quote on my bathroom wall so I can read it every day.

> *Every day think as you wake up,*
> *Today I am fortunate to have woken up,*
> *I am alive, I have a precious human life.*
> *I am not going to waste it.*
> *I am going to use*
> *All my energies to develop myself.*
> *To expand my heart out to others.*
> *To achieve enlightenment for*
> *The benefit of all beings.*
> *I am going to have kind*

> *Thoughts toward others.*
> *I am not going to get angry*
> *Or think badly about others.*
> *I am going to benefit others*
> *As much as I can.*
> — His Holiness the 14th Dalai Lama

There is a problem with being a "trained" mind versus a mind that takes joy in constantly learning. The problem with being trained is that the techniques and knowledge will surely become dated in time. The ideal practitioner has the willingness constantly to be aware of the improvements available in medical research and will gleefully take the necessary steps to understand the changes because he or she understands that being perfectly knowledgeable about any given topic is unachievable. New techniques and approaches are born all the time. It's important to know that your teachers cannot teach you everything, but they can teach you enough from their experiences and perspectives to give you a foundation to build upon. Work hard constantly to "update" your knowledge instead of working hard to perfect it.

> *The mind best fitted for survival in any world is the mind that has discovered how knowledge can be joyful, leading to a friendship with wisdom that is pure delight. That mind is ready to tackle any kind of knowledge with intentness of will.*
> — Northrop Frye

Virtually, thousands of ways exist to improve yourself, to seek knowledge, and to achieve your goals with clear intent. The way I have found that works the best for me is taking as many classes as I can, listening to my coach and mentors, and finding a way to donate my time or money to charity and my community.

BE AWARD-WINNING

A local newspaper here in the Seattle area publishes the local "top businesspeople." What it doesn't say is that those businesspeople often paid well to be listed as top people. A local TV channel does it much better; it accepts nominations from businesses and then people vote via its website. Some businesses aggressively promote their campaign to be named the top business and they ask for testimonials from their employees, clients, and patients. However, I have heard of this scenario backfiring on a business when its employees and patients did not have such nice things to say.

Faking that you're award-winning is the quickest way to lose an immense amount of respect in the health profession. While such claims may fool plenty of patients, be certain that many others will not be fooled but see right through the award as a scam. Legitimate awards come from donating your time selflessly to the benefit of others, doing something nobody else has done, and standing out from the crowd by being uniquely you. Ask your mentors or coach which organizational awards are legitimate and whether you should consider applying for them or working toward getting them.

A way to become award-winning is to focus on incremental goals. Check in with yourself often and ask yourself what you are doing to improve your skills now. Don't always put off self-improvement. What you are doing to improve is a great way to start a conversation. People are always impressed by other people who constantly work to improve themselves. Also, improvements are not always made by adding new things, but often, they are about refining what skills you have. Contact your professional association or school to learn about awards you may be able to pursue, and then contact the organizations giving out the awards to learn the criteria. Once you know the criteria, strive toward fulfilling and achieving the award—now you have a new lofty goal to pursue to set a higher standard for yourself.

> *It doesn't matter how fast you are moving toward your goals.*
> *The key is that you are moving toward your goals steadily, on a daily basis, because, over time, this daily involvement will add up and produce results. Each daily action, no matter how small, will bring you one step closer to your destiny.*
> ~Patrick Snow, bestselling author of *Creating Your Own Destiny*

MEASURE YOUR SUCCESS

Story Time:

On one consulting engagement, I was assigned to work under a highly experienced Business Intelligence Architect to build a business intelligence strategy for a very large corporation. The company had assigned us to figure out its strategic goals and ways to measure them using an automated system it could access easily via the web. While figuring out these organizational goals, we interviewed all the stakeholders involved in making determinations of what the organization's priorities were, and then we assembled a long list of priorities for the organization based on their feedback. During this project, I learned that most people in an organization often do not understand what is most important about their work and how it relates to the business' objectives.

After the strategy to build this elaborate, automated business intelligence system was designed, key figures in the operation worked

> *very hard to stop its implementation. Measuring their success was the hardest task to ask them to do in the end because there were plenty of people who didn't want to reveal where they were at in achieving their part of the overall goals. Burying your head in the sand and not paying attention to what is most important only does a disservice to yourself and makes your job harder. Not knowing exactly how your business is doing because you're not measuring is like sailing a ship blindfolded.*

Have you ever worked for an organization that loved to state its goals for the organization, but you had no idea how your role played a part in that goal? This problem is very common for many organizations large and small.

In *Four Disciplines of Execution*, Stephen Covey provides a roadmap to working more effectively toward our goals. Here is a summary of his steps to achieve goals more efficiently:

1. Figure out what is the most important goal of all and focus on that. These are the goals that must be achieved or nothing else matters. Humans are wired to do only one thing really well at a time, and often do a bunch of things together with mediocrity.

2. Create a way to measure your success visibly on working toward this goal. It makes you more organized on how you will achieve it. It will give you the opportunity to go back daily to keep you focused on your goal. Plan weekly as a team or by yourself if you're on your own.

3. Translate those extremely important goals into specific actions and replicate times when you've done something

well. Once you find a new and even better way to achieve these goals, you repeat these actions until you reach your goal consistently. Knowing what your goal is and what to do about it are two very different things.

4. Remember that your patients, or your coworkers, and your fellow health care practitioners are counting on you. When we know we are being held accountable for our work to someone, we provide better service to our patients and clients and find more value in our work.

I've read some business books about building a practice that say you should get your measuring down to "profit per hour." While I think the hourly profit can be a very revealing measure, there is such a thing as spending too much time measuring. Time is your most precious asset, and you do not want to waste it trying to measure something that won't do much to build your business. Choose measures that don't cost you a lot of time, energy, or money; otherwise, you will lose your focus on where you should be spending these resources.

Focus on the most important thing—your productivity. Being productive and being busy are two different things. Many offices I've visited are enormously busy, but far from productive. One particular office has trouble keeping up with the demands of its business. The business' patients know their bills will be late, and they have come to realize how disorganized the office is by how many mistakes often happen with their billing. Everyone is running around like a chicken with its head cut off and the patients have noticed. Appointments run late and the patients get agitated and often take it out on the front desk receptionist who is just trying to keep the phone from ringing uncontrollably.

What this office could do to improve this situation is to have everyone focus his or her energy on the most important things by level in the organization and what each person has to contribute to the overall goal. The biller should not be distracted with other management-related decisions—she should focus on billing. The front desk people should not be bothered with an assortment of time-wasting busy work—they should focus on making the customer experience as enjoyable as possible, and if necessary, get another staff member just to answer the phones. The doctors should not be distracted with other items on their "To Do" lists while they are seeing patients—they should budget their time so they have time to deal with small practice items that do not relate to the time they spend with patients so the patients never feel rushed or poorly taken care of because the doctor is too busy.

KEY LESSONS:

- Stay up to date on your skills.
- Strive for real awards and avoid the fake ones.
- Measure your successes.

Part 2

PREVENTING BURNOUT— HAVE WORK-LIFE BALANCE

Chapter 6

UNDERSTANDING YOUR LIMITATIONS

Chapter Summary: Sometimes people go way too far when they start out. Be realistic with what you feel your body and mind can handle. Avoid getting a bad case of "contact overload" by getting time alone. Lead a balanced life by structuring your schedule.

BE REALISTIC

> *Story Time:*
>
> *One panel I served on as a speaker to a class of new graduates from massage school had a fascinating massage therapist who had been seeing forty patients a week for some time. Her story was grand with how much income she was achieving, how much word-of-mouth she was generating, and the great results her career had brought to her life. Part of her story, though, was about when she simply turned her head to view a clock that was behind her and tore her trapezius muscle in the process, thus making her unable to continue her work during the long period of time it took to heal. After she healed, she went back to seeing that incredible number of patients—most likely because she had been used to the income level it brought to her. Unfortunately, her body had already told her she might not be able to do that kind of volume forever.*

Many of us come out of school with grand visions of how many patients we will want to see in a week. Some of us even think we'll throw open our business doors and people will line up to get in. While it is great to dream, such grand visions can mislead us about our potential income and drive us to burnout trying to achieve it. The important lesson here is to consider the source where you heard that seeing that many patients was possible.

> *Story Time:*
>
> *An example of someone who has balanced her work and personal life well is a highly successful naturopath who has a popular radio show, a thriving practice, and a long history of being a very effective practitioner at what she does. She has structured her hours around her family's needs, only takes a limited number of patients, and does not deviate from her scheduled work hours. New patients sometimes have trouble getting in for months because she is so busy, but she does not deviate from her schedule to accommodate—she knows her limitations and sticks with them. What this schedule has done is make her appear as in demand as she really is. She has no problem keeping to her schedule limitations because she has done it this way for many years; she knows if she exceeds those boundaries, then she will have to give up something else in her life—like time with her family. While her chosen style of practice is not physically intensive, she acknowledges the need to limit the amount of time she allows herself to be available to others to avoid burnout.*

INTROVERTS—HIGHLY SENSITIVE PEOPLE

Many people in health care often face what is called "Contact Overload" because of how many people they need to interface with during any given day. Often, individuals in health care could be classified as "Highly Sensitive People" or HSP's. This trait is found in 15-20 percent of all people and makes them more prone to Contact Overload or anxiety when dealing with other people. Being an HSP is not a weakness—it is a trait to be honed into a valuable skill.

> *Story Time:*
>
> *A great friend of mine, Cori Kruger, LMP, was born in the country and loves her extremely small hometown. Upon becoming a practitioner, she realized she needed to practice in a more populated area to make ends meet. Upon driving into the city every day, she realized how much of a toll it took on her psyche, so she schedules time in the mountains for herself on a regular basis to put herself back in her comfort zone and recharge her spirit for the next week.*

When I recognized that I too was an HSP, I took steps to remedy my anxiety by hiring a hypnotherapist, Marie Maguire, MA, CMS, CHt, FIBH. In just three sessions, we addressed my anxiety. I am now much more confident and at ease in social and speaking situations, and I can honestly say that working with Marie was life-changing. There are many ways to deal with anxiety, but for me, seeing Marie was the easiest and most effective in the long-term.

A lot of quick tips exist to "jump start your visibility" if you're an introvert like so many other health practitioners. Most of these ideas boil down to one main point: introverts need to learn to balance the time they spend being introspective about what they will do with their time against productively using the time they have to accomplish what needs to be done. Too often, people get caught in the cycle of thinking that busy means productive, but in reality, that is far from the case.

Work hard to understand what you are good at and acknowledge your successes. The best way to do so is to take a few moments to write down and take stock in what you've done well. Consider the patients you've helped along the way so far. Learn to articulate your successes really well to others. A good way to get good at articulating your successes is to bounce them off your mentors or coaches for feedback.

After you have met someone, reach out to him or her to continue the relationship. I can't tell you how many times I've left this step out because I got busy doing something else and I sincerely regretted later that I didn't do it. If you don't follow up within about a twenty-four hour period, it is likely that the interaction's value may get lost along the way and you will probably forget to follow up. Learn to make it a habit to send an introduction email after a meeting, and add the person's contact information to your list of professional contacts. My routine is to send an introduction email and add the person to my professional network on LinkedIn to keep track of him or her. Many other networking websites are available, but this one seems to have the most people I know already on it.

Another great way to learn to put yourself out there is to watch a master extrovert. While that person may be doing things that don't resonate with you, try to put your own spin onto his or approach. When necessary, soft spoken individuals like me can still get the same job done that a master extrovert can do. I model my approach after an incredible extrovert chiropractor I admire, Dr. Stefan Black, DC. It is because of him, and observing many other wildly successful extroverts, that I have learned to put my agenda out there at meetings, volunteer for projects that will give me more visibility, and put myself out there even if I'm afraid I'll be made a fool. Chances are nine out of ten people will love me, and I take those chances more often because of the examples extroverts have given me. Just because you may be an introvert now, don't discount the example that many extroverts can give us to think about and possibly apply to our lives to change our reality.

STRUCTURE YOUR HOURS—TIME MANAGEMENT

> *Story Time:*
>
> *At one point in my career, I had a home-based practice where I often saw many of my close friends as clients. They loved having the opportunity to come over and hang out for a bit while we meandered to getting to the treatment session. The appointment times became in flux and many of my fantastic friends would be late for their appointments since "it was just at my house."*
>
> *While it was lovely to have them around when they did arrive, it made it intensely difficult for me to keep up on the other aspects of my business like my bookkeeping, my paperwork, and my various marketing projects. I often had to stay up until the wee hours of the morning to catch up with my work; that and other reasons ultimately made me decide to shut down my home practice and set up better boundaries around my work times. I loved my friends just too much and couldn't bring myself to rein in the times when I was at home. But when I was at the office, a clear boundary was set that I was on a tight schedule and didn't have as much time to socialize, which allowed me to regain some of my work-life balance.*

From the lesson I learned above, I decided to structure my schedule according to what most of my patients would like to have and what I could feasibly commit to in a given week. I now have two successful offices where, at each, I practice part-time. I take no more than twenty appointments a week, which meets my modest needs for income and my body's increasing desire for a lighter workload than I have done in the past. Based on the requests coming in from clients, I've decided that evening hours are when most of my patients are available, and I cut Saturdays from my schedule because they weren't nearly as popular as I expected. Then I set these hours on my online scheduler for my patients, who understand those are the hours I'm available and I cannot deviate from them. The reasons why I cannot deviate from them are not only to prevent a repeat injury like I had before, but also, my wish to create stability and structure in my life so I know when I will be working at my office and which office I will be at on any given day so I can structure errands and other appointments around those hours. I found that having a schedule that is constantly in flux frustrates patients, and it can show that I do not have the work-life balance I try to teach them about. It's important to practice what we preach about having that balance, and having a structured schedule is the best way I've found to accomplish that for myself.

> *No matter which planner you use, it's essential that you apply the 'select one' rule: making it the one and only place where you record all your activities, appointments, and things to do.... Your planner becomes an extension of you.*
> — Julie Morgenstern, *Time Management from the Inside Out: The Foolproof System for Taking Control of Your Schedule—and Your Life*

To keep all these networking meetings, personal appointments, my two practice locations, and my relationship going during this time, I have always employed as many effective tools as I possibly can that are NOT paper based. Paper is the antithesis of organization, so you need to learn to move on if you have a romance with paper. I have a calendar on my cell phone and an associated task list, which I follow religiously; they synchronize with the web, so if I ever lose my cell phone, I'll still have all my appointments, and I highly recommend you learn to adopt a similar system. My online schedulers for my practices synchronize with my phone and keep down how many appointments I have to enter in my phone.

It can change your life to be amazingly organized. If you have time management issues, consider taking a class on time management, or take the time to learn from someone who is better at it than you are.

> *Story Time:*
>
> *Several years ago, I pushed myself beyond my capabilities, and to this day, I continue to pay a hefty price for doing so. As the manager of the massage department for two extremely high volume group practices, I had a team of twelve therapists working under me. Meeting my manager's demands for my team, running my own practice within the clinics, and filling in for therapists who called in sick proved to be a disastrous combination for my left shoulder and wrist. As many people in my profession often do when they work far too much, I developed a very painful case of Thoracic Outlet Syndrome in my shoulder and Carpal Tunnel Syndrome in my wrist. In my desperation to reduce my workload, I left this*

> *practice for a "simpler life"—being an independent contractor at another clinic filling in for a therapist who had been in a car accident. It was my thinking that calming down my responsibilities would reduce the enormous amount of pain to a manageable level. Unfortunately, I was wrong and I needed to take a long hiatus from my work in order for my shoulder and wrist to heal to the level where I could continue my work again.*
>
> *During this time away from my work, I was horribly depressed, feeling so far off from my life's purpose, even though I had a great second career in consulting. Massage is my life's passion, and while I can do other things quite well, it was deviating from what I felt was my life's purpose that drove me to the breaking point. I learned that I may not have had this forced break in my career if I had taken better care of myself, acknowledged my limitations, and not said, "Yes" to every request that was made of me.*

GETTING HELP

If you want to magnify your possibilities, you're going to need a hand to execute your plans. If you think you can't afford help in the office, think again and look at some creative options. You can find help via many freelancers often at reasonable prices. My suggestion would be to be very clear on exactly what you want the freelancer to accomplish instead of waiting for him to ask you lots of probing questions—just be pleasantly surprised when he does. Most freelancers expect you to have a clear idea of what you are hiring them to do. On Health Care Professionals Referrals Networking's website, www.hcprn.org, you can find a suggested list of websites where you can hire a freelancer who could be anywhere in the world. Always pay very close attention to the portfolios and ratings of the freelancers; they will be looking very closely at your ratings as well.

Internships are an excellent way to get cost-effective help for your business venture. I suggest you not be on an extremely tight timetable because the process to get an intern can be lengthy. You should have some knowledge of what it is you're asking the intern to do, but give some trust to the person's expertise to bring you the rest of the way. Most interns are students who desperately need the experience—so you don't have to offer them a paid internship all the time. If you have more than one intern, ask them to check each other's work before it's presented to you to save you time.

The economy greatly affects how well unpaid internships do, so keep this in mind if you're not getting any responses on your unpaid internships. Need a website built? Hire a student studying graphic design and websites. Need someone to help with a marketing project? Hire a student studying marketing or someone in school to learn your profession.

You can try a lot of different ways to get interns to help with business projects, so don't limit yourself solely to working the maze of the colleges to find their internship coordinators. You can simply Google "free internship posting" and post your internship opening on a number of sites at no cost. This wider audience for your posting should give you a better chance of getting applicants.

To have an internship at your office, go to local schools' career services departments and inquire who their internship coordinators are. They will provide you with the means to get the word out to students. Remember, the key with mentoring interns and anyone else is patience and openness. You want your interns to get the most out of working with you so they will talk highly of their experiences with others.

Here is a sample internship advertisement to send to internship coordinators and post online:

POSITION: HCPRN Website Internship

General Information

- The Web Department offers internships year-round on a rolling basis.

- Length of internship and hours per week are negotiable, although we prefer interns to be available for the mornings on business days on a combination of weekdays (M/W/F, T/Th, or M-F). We have a Monday morning conference call at 9 a.m. that is mandatory—attendance at all other scheduled events and meetings can be negotiated.

- Interns must stay for the length of a semester or summer.

- This is an unpaid internship.

- We will work with schools for student interns receiving credit, but receiving credit is not required.

- Interns are assigned a mentor who will work with the selected candidate to establish learning objectives to develop skills in the intern's chosen area.

Requirements

Students or recent graduates of any social media, publicity, English, literature, marketing, and advertising program are encouraged. The ideal candidates are familiar with different and constantly evolving technologies, and have some experience and/or education related to web and/or IT technologies. Must be able to work independently and persistently on intern projects. Must have excellent organization and communications skills. Must own your own laptop and have access to the internet and a phone line for virtual work.

Description

The Web Intern will assist website and marketing staff with a number of projects to support the organization's websites including:

- Coordination and uploading of new text, image and media content to the HCPRN websites

- Assist in conducting research

- Assist in special department projects as needed

Application Process

Interested students should email their resume and cover letter, expressing their qualifications and interest in the internship to: dene@nwpainrelief.com. The subject line should read: ATTN: HCRPN Website Internship

Candidates may also fax their resumes to (888) 823-7381 or mail to:

Health Care Professionals Referral Networking (HCPRN)
Attn: HCPRN Website Internship
9415 Roosevelt Way NE
Seattle, WA 98115

Candidates who are believed to be a good match will then be invited to complete an online application and come in for an interview.

KEY LESSONS:

- Don't overdo it.

- Get a regular dose of time alone to recharge.

- Stick to a structured schedule.

- Use your resources; get some help when you need it.

Chapter 7

SELF-CARE

Chapter Summary: Even when you're rigid on self-care, you might just be leaving something out. If your body starts to tell you something, listen to it and keep searching for that missing piece that will keep you going strong. Use your network to get the care you need while you build relationships through trades, but be careful not to enter into too many trades or get caught up in a bad one. Plan your time off as far in advance as possible and give your patients plenty of other options for practitioners to see while you're gone.

> *Story Time:*
>
> *Prior to my painful injury to my shoulder and wrist, I thought I was doing enough self-care with chiropractic, massage, acupuncture, and a rigorous stretching routine. I was a regular at my chiropractor and received at least one massage a week, and I added on acupuncture, as my acupuncturist felt was necessary. I thought that doing all this self-care would prove to be enough to allow me to keep my high volume schedule of around thirty patients a week. After my injury, I realized that simply doing these steps for self-care was not enough. I forgot a critical component—body mechanics.*

> *What I should have done was schedule an occasional consultation with one of my previous instructors to check in with how I was conducting myself during a session and moving my body. We think that when we get out of school we're still fresh on what we're supposed to be doing so we'll keep doing our work right. Unfortunately, this is not true and we need to check in with our instructors to make sure we are still doing our work right. Another such way I could have incorporated body mechanics coaching was to take a class on body mechanics. Because of this hard lesson, the support group I run, Northwest LMP Support Group, is always looking for instructors who teach body mechanics to come in and demo their courses. Hindsight is 20/20, and I wish I had listened to my better judgment because, to this day, I still fight these injuries to keep my career.*

TRADING YOUR WAY TO A HEALTHIER YOU

A great way to get all this self-care is by doing trades with other practitioners where you do your work on one another. Most practitioners will graciously help out a fellow injured practitioner as a part of professional courtesy. If they are too busy or in need of income, they probably won't be able to help, but plenty of people are willing.

Be cautious of scheduling too many trades because you will soon find they fill up your schedule quickly and leave little time for you actually to earn an income. Also, by not putting boundaries around when you can trade and how often, you will find yourself in a predicament of having to cancel these trades when they begin to become too much. Graciously thanking the person who wants to trade and telling him or her that you need to open up that time for income is a good way to handle it. Be cautious of being too urgent with cancelling these sessions because it can make you appear unpredictable to another practitioner. Always give the other practitioner plenty of notice, or set the expectation that your appointment is tentative if another client wants the time.

If you're in the process of doing a trade and you find that your trading partner isn't exactly what you expected, gracefully bow out of the trade. The best way is to explain that you aren't able to accommodate the trade in your schedule at the moment, but you will keep him or her in mind when more time opens up for trades. Be careful not to offend the practitioner, as you can ruin a valuable relationship.

Story Time:

A massage therapist offered a trade to another practitioner at a class just to be friendly. This practitioner took her up on it awhile later and looked forward to this session with her. When she arrived, she was haggard looking and clearly was not in a good space. During the session, they quickly realized that the style of work was not quite what she wanted to get. During the session, the massage recipient barked, "More pressure!" over and over again. The therapist felt she was using a generous amount of pressure already and didn't want to exceed her capabilities just to satisfy the recipient's desire for more.

The interaction was kind of painful. Unfortunately, the therapist who was receiving the massage reflected a demeanor that ruined a possible referral relationship because now it is known she can be not very personable. Remember to be polite and honest at the same time—you'll win more flies with honey than with hydrochloric acid. Trades can make or break a referral relationship.

In an effort to continue my chiropractic care, which I find essential to keeping my body moving along, I made an arrangement to provide ongoing business coaching to my chiropractor. He has the ability to contact me anytime with any question he wants to pick my brain about, and in return, he keeps my body tuned up for my work. It's a win-win and a fantastic way to trade.

Trades can prove beneficial for filling in the gaps in your skills—such as the chiropractor has done with me to fill in business advice needs—I consider such trades as part of a self-care routine because they can remove the stress of a weakness, which by itself can drive you to madness if not properly addressed. I believe the chiropractor has had a similar arrangement in the past for a landscaper, a computer guy, and a few other household things. Finding someone who is willing to barter can be tricky because he or she may not be of the highest quality, so consider very carefully whom you are taking on for the trade. It can prove extremely smart to write down the expectations of the barter arrangement.

Story Time:

One therapist told me about her experience with a trade: "I wished I had clearly defined what my expectations of a barter trade were when my business partner and I hired a consultant to come give us fresh ideas for marketing our practice. We had hit a stalling point in our growth and counted on this person to bring us the magic bullet we had been seeking. The mistake I made was to offer up the trade too quickly without further checking the person's references and success ratios from her clients. Unfortunately, this marketing consultant didn't have enough experience in building a health care practice and lacked the understanding of the tight budget we were on for our advertising. This lack of experience

> *proved to be the downfall of the consulting arrangement as she brought a lot of strategies we had already tried that could easily be found by searching the web, or we did not have the resources to try, or they were a hefty price we didn't expect. We should have written down our expectations and how much the arrangement was going to cost in the long run prior to making the deal."*

PLANNING FOR TIME OFF

A very important component of self-care is time off to take care of your family. Throughout my career, I have worked evenings to accommodate the schedules of most of my potential patients. Because my partner worked days, our schedules conflicted so it was difficult to get time to see each other during the workweek. To balance myself, I planned out vacations and time with my partner to rekindle our connection. It's important to take care of your relationship health along with your personal health.

When you're planning for time off, it's important to schedule far in advance. I personally try to schedule all my time off at the beginning of the year so I can input these dates in my online scheduler. To the clients, my online schedule looks like I am booked the days I plan to take off, so they usually just select another time. If they are talking to me in person, I merely say, "I'm sorry; I'm booked that day." This practice keeps me from cancelling my vacation, which I have done in the past to meet a client's needs. If you have clients who are in desperate need of help during the time you are away, arrange a list of alternate practitioners in the area to help them. Most likely they will not go to these alternates because they have developed a relationship of trust with you already, but it shows you have plenty of confidence in the value you provide while you have concern that your patients will get the treatment they need.

When I'm planning to have extended time off, I always schedule my clients ahead for the week I get back from my time off. I've found that this practice ensures that you're busy when you get back from vacation and it keeps the patient's treatment plan on track better than just saying, "I'm going to be out of town next week, so I'll catch up with you when I get back." This general statement has proven over and over to be a bad idea because usually what happens is a lag in getting people to reschedule simply because you've fallen off their radar for the moment.

> *Story Time:*
>
> *A great friend of mine was pregnant with her next child. She knew she would be taking an extended maternity leave after the birth. In this case, she didn't know when she would be back, so she contacted the trusted people in her network she knew would honor that she was sending her clients their way and asked their permission to pass their information along to her patients. She provided a list of recommended providers in the area, a short description of each of their specialties, contact information for each of them, and a map showing the locations of their offices. She then gave this information to every patient when she was coming close to her due date. Her patients might not have visited these providers, but at the very least, they felt she tried to make sure they could get the care they needed. She knew when she returned from her maternity leave that it was likely some patients would have moved on, but others would happily return to hear all about her new baby and to resume the connection they had created with her as a practitioner.*

This same rule applies when you're out sick for a day or two. Make sure to present options to your patients for other providers in the area or your office. Talk to the other provider and get his permission to give out his information—this step may save your patients time and frustration if that provider is already too busy to take them. Try to cancel as far in advance as you can, and if you cancel with less than twenty-four hours notice, give the patient a "get out of jail free" opportunity when he or she has to cancel on you. This flexibility will help you to build a relationship with the client—the client knows you're reliable and will trust you always to be.

KEY LESSONS:

- If you think you're doing enough self-care, you're probably not—be careful and listen to your body.

- Trades are a great way to get the care you need.

- Be careful of too many trades or bad trades.

- Plan your time off far in advance.

- Give your patients other options if you're going to be absent from your practice.

Chapter 8

DEALING WITH ADVERSITY

Chapter Summary: Not busy enough? Check in with your mentor or coach and get a second opinion on the way you're doing things. Don't make insurance companies your primary source of income, and especially, don't rely on just one of them. When you're having trouble with money, be honest with yourself and any business partners so problems don't come as a huge surprise to anyone. If you're under the weather in your career, seek out a support group for your profession and spend time with your peers to get recharged. Acknowledge your accomplishments and don't beat yourself up for what you haven't yet achieved.

JUST NOT BUSY ENOUGH

When you start out, if you work for a busy practice, even if it gives you a delicious prime shift on its schedule, the patients haven't met you, so you need to help them by earning their trust and teaching them to value your techniques. It will most likely take time for your schedule to fill, and even if it's full the day you walk in, you want to give those clients a very good reason to reschedule with you. If they find they are mistreated in any way, no matter how busy the clinic, you will quickly find you aren't as busy as the other people on staff.

> *Life is like mountain climbing. Fulfillment is achieved by relentless dedication to the ascent, sometimes slow, painful step, by slow painful step.*
> — Paul G. Stoltz, *Adversity Quotient: Turning Obstacles into Opportunities*

Try to get to the root of the matter of why you're not busy. Are you not promoting your skills properly? Do you need someone to help you change some bad habits? Is your technique for your approach lacking?

Don't sit there and mope about your lack of success—remember that if there's time to complain, there's time to fix the problem. Gather feedback from mentors and coaches if possible and learn from your weaknesses so you can be successful. Ask them to role-play with you your full interaction with a patient and to give you feedback about your approach. Make sure you get the most brutally honest people to tell you the truth about your manner—good friends are not always a great choice for this job since they want to be polite most of the time. Keep those good friends for inspiration when you are down, but use the brutally honest people close to you to tell you the truth.

A DEAL WITH THE DEVIL: INSURANCE COMPANIES

If you do not accept insurance, you may be excluding a large number of people from your possible income. However, accepting insurance is something I think of as "making a deal with the devil." You lower your rates by agreeing to contract with the company. It means more exposure to potential clients, but it also introduces the risk of forbearing payment, which does not always mean you will be paid.

> *Story Time:*
>
> *Some insurance companies will flood you with patients, which can present an entirely new problem. A massage therapist I knew had a thriving practice of her own full of patients from one insurance company. She was making decent money and had just bought herself a condominium and a new car. Unfortunately, she was not a very organized person and the insurance company audited her. When she had trouble coming up with requested documentation, they stopped all payment to her. She was instantly bankrupt because they had become her primary income source.*

If you do decide to accept insurance, make sure no one insurance company is your primary source of income. Diversify your income between cash and insurance patients to spread your risk. If you have trouble with any one insurance company, you will not have as great an issue because you will still have other sources of income continuing until the problem is resolved.

Knowing that I had to measure my goals and productivity, and not be too dependent on any one revenue stream, I drew upon my skills to create a really small scale business intelligence strategy on the cheap, using free tools available online for my practice. I used an online bookkeeping solution that gave me vivid visual charts and data-driven databases that would tell me who were my best customers, my different types of revenue streams, my income and expenses, and my biggest vendors. I could tell if my practice was becoming too dependent on one insurance company and cautiously scheduled new patients from a company that appeared to be taking up most of my schedule or giving me a tough time getting payment on other patients.

TOUGH FINANCIAL TIMES

> *Story Time:*
>
> *One therapist I knew was going through some tough financial times because the business was not growing as fast as she had hoped. Her business partner never really complained, but she wasn't busy either. It was hard, but she had to tell her business partner that only a couple of months of money were left for her. While telling a business partner this information may seem very personal, the truth is it is much better to let your business partner know where you're at and to be authentic than to hide the situation until the last moment when the business collapses under the strain of expenses.*
>
> *The right thing to do when you realize you are in this situation is to look for another source of supplemental income and not wait to find it. Many small business owners find themselves needing another stable source of income while starting their practices. It can be a very stressful time for anyone when a business owner realizes he or she has to scale back from full-time.*

In his book *Safe Money in Tough Times: Everything You Need to Know to Survive the Financial Crisis*, Jonathan Pond says, "Tough financial times need not be a totally negative experience, however. Because our financial lives are unsettled during an uncertain economy, we are forced to take a closer look at the way we manage and spend our money."

The next thing to do would be to start a surge of new marketing programs. Brainstorm between partners on new things to do to promote the business that won't cost you money. If you don't have a business partner, attend a local support group to get a fresh influx of new ideas. Contact your association to find out if there may be a group running nearby.

Patrick Snow, author of *The Affluent Entrepreneur: 20 Proven Principles for Achieving Prosperity*, notes, "Whether you realize it or not, you have everything you need to address any and all adversities you face." Don't panic, don't freak out, don't go cry in a corner. Get your thinking cap on. Mom always yelled, "Concentrate!" to me as I left the house each day to go to school. I used to think my mother was really weird to do that every day, but then, as I got older, I got it—she wanted me to remember to think things through.

Whatever you do, avoid taking out loans, and don't lean on someone else for income support for too long. It can build a situation of remorse between partners, families, and friends. When you're running out of money, do the wise thing and create a new income stream to help you keep your business running while it's getting back on its feet. Yes, I said that—get a supplemental job. To return to a previous field temporarily to keep you going in your health care profession is really not admitting a failure; it's keeping you moving toward your dream.

SUPPORT GROUPS WORK WONDERS

Support groups for professionals, also called "peer supervision groups," are extremely helpful when conducted well. When I started the Northwest LMP Support Group, it was our mission to help raise money for the Massage Therapy Foundation while creating a way to keep massage therapists in their careers longer. At the group meetings, we use our collective experience to answer questions and support each other through issues. We run study groups for students getting ready for their licensing exams to help foster new people into our profession with a built-in support network for them from the start.

When starting a support group, consider calling on your association. Remember that some associations may have chapter meetings, which they consider their version of a support group. While some of these chapter meetings may have an atmosphere of support, most often, they are not places where people seeking support would feel comfortable revealing truths about how their careers are going. Here is where you have the golden opportunity to create something fresh and new. I've seen support groups that charge their members, but I've also seen that sometimes those types of setups don't last. Support needs to be available to the members who can't afford to go anywhere else for help. In my opinion, the best kind of support is free, but it's fine to collect a donation for a greater cause. When we hold our meetings for the Northwest LMP Support Group, we pass around an envelope for donations to the Massage Therapy Foundation. Some people donate, others do not—it doesn't matter—it's about working toward the greater cause. As an added bonus, some of the time spent with the group can sometimes be counted as Continuing Education Credits for the participants. Check with your profession's administrating Department of Health to find out whether you can count hours at a group like this for Continuing Education Credits as well.

Social media is a great way to start a group in your area. Some very successful groups have been started on Facebook and they have grown rapidly. Our group used Meetup.com, which has proven to be an excellent method to get the word out, organize meetings, and keep in touch with members. I have read books that encourage you to do a mailing or post advertisements, which I would highly recommend. Some associations will do a mailing on your behalf at no charge while others may not even respond to your request—call upon your resources before spending money on starting a group. If you are organized, use technology effectively, and call on your network. Creating and maintaining a group should take less than ten hours a month of your time and should not become your main focus.

APPRECIATING WHAT YOU HAVE

> *Peaks are moments when you appreciate what you have. Valleys are moments when you long for what is missing.*
> — Spencer Johnson, *Peaks and Valleys: Making Good and Bad Times Work for You—At Work And In Life*

Most small business people are goal-oriented people and most goal-oriented people are dreamers. Sometimes we become so critical of ourselves that we beat ourselves down over the things we visualized that haven't materialized yet. Many times in my career, I have run into people who are wildly successful in their own right, but failed to notice it themselves.

> *Story Time:*
>
> *A therapist writes, "A massage therapist I once worked with briefly had an amazing space on the beach where she had a steady and loyal, fun-loving clientele built almost entirely on word-of-mouth. Her space was ideal and was probably what many people who would love to work for themselves would dream of as their perfect space. When she walked around her space, she saw all the flaws. When she looked at her schedule, she felt she wasn't busy enough. Eventually, she succumbed to all this self-imposed stress and fell into a period of despair. I left my brief period of working with this therapist too fast and in the wrong way. In hindsight, I wish I could have supported her better and helped her get through that hard time, but instead, I left terribly and lost a potential great friend in my profession."*

Sometimes we need to sit back for a moment to realize that we have accomplished amazing things—sometimes these accomplishments are what others would dream of their whole lives and never do. Take stock in your surroundings and pay yourself the respect of knowing how successful you already are. Then be gentle with yourself when pursuing your ultimate goals, and don't break yourself down for the little flaws in your world that you see around you. Celebrate your successes and savor them—even the small ones.

KEY LESSONS:

- Be cautious of having too much of any one income stream that is dependent upon payment from any one particular insurance company.

- Be honest with any business partners about your current financial status.

- Join a support group when times get tough. If there isn't one, make one.

- Take stock in what you have done so far and don't beat yourself up.

Chapter 9

DEALING WITH INJURIES

Chapter Summary: Being injured is one of the most helpless feelings you can have as a practitioner. Being unable to do your work can have a profound effect on your psyche and relationships. Your health care practitioner friends are often willing to be there for you—just ask and get some help when you need it. Structure your schedule to allow for a budgeted amount of work every week so you don't overdo it.

WHEN I HURT MYSELF

With a team of twelve practitioners working for me, I was greatly rewarded by watching them become more and more successful using the procedures and techniques I had taught them. I felt inspired every single day I came to work by them, and sadly disappointed whenever a practitioner was not successful. Just as many practitioners were working hard as those who were not working hard. I only wanted "go-getters" on my team, so I had to let go of quite a few people who didn't make the cut when they were given the opportunity. This turnover took its toll on my psyche and my body because I was often filling in for those folks who decided not to show up for work or I had to let go. Also there were plenty of times when people who were doing well just got sick or needed to take a vacation. In an effort to keep my manager happy with the overall productivity of the group, I often took on patients to fill in for others, which became my downfall.

The pain started slowly as a burning sensation in my left shoulder; then it creeped into my neck. Next, I noticed a tingling sensation in my left hand, then a searing nerve like pain that went from my left armpit and into my hand. It felt like a tourniquet was wrapped around my arm. As a professional in the field of massage, I knew these symptoms were not a good sign and could signal the end of my career in the style of hands-on work I practiced if I didn't take time to rest and recuperate. The problem was that my duties as a manager would not rest, so I was pushed on to continue the actions that created the problem.

When the pain became so great, I knew it was time to see my medical doctor. He said to me, "You have thoracic outlet syndrome in your shoulder and carpal tunnel syndrome in your wrist. You need to stop doing massage now." This statement was a devastating blow to me because my profession in massage therapy had become my identity and what I thought would be my life's work.

Thinking that if I just decreased my workload and worked as a therapist only, I would slowly heal, I left management of those practices and switched jobs to work for a therapist who had been in an auto accident and needed someone to take over her client base. Sadly, my shoulder completely gave way about six months into this work, so I had to bow out. The pain had reached such unbearable levels that I was forced to find work unrelated to my passion but based on my other abilities. While working in something other than my calling, I was forced to squelch my desires to continue that work.

My partner had urged me to move on from thinking that doing bodywork was even an option since the doctor had told me I could no longer continue at it. I became grumpy, high maintenance, and hard to live with due to all the pain. Thinking my career was already over before I had even paid off my student loans sucked me into a deep depression. My relationship equally deteriorated during this time of pain and depression.

I still remember a day when I was in a meeting as a consultant for a major corporation. The task at hand was extremely important, but I couldn't help noticing a lady sitting across from me who was rubbing her neck. I saw her and I wanted so badly to stand up and tell her, "I can help with that!" but my shoulder, arm, and hand throbbed with the pain of simply doing the work in front of me on a computer. After that meeting, I went to the ladies room to take a moment to breathe; instead, I cried in the bathroom stall of this gigantic corporation. So many people would have sold their souls to be working there, but I was miserable feeling that my life's purpose had been ripped from me, and I was stuck there being a slave to this machine. It was then I realized that somehow, someday, I would be back doing the work I loved, and that this time was merely a way to get me there.

During this time, I really remembered that my friends were there to help me—all I had to do was ask. When I was in school, a small ganglion cyst developed in the joint of my ring finger on my left hand, making it hard to grip things. I knew another student had dropped out of the program because of the same problem. It was worrying me to no end, and I didn't really know what

I should do. It was then that I came to my instructor and mentor, Zdenka Daucik, LMP, and asked her for her help. Zdenka was unorthodox and I respected her aggressive approach to problems. She took my hand, made two quick movements, and said "there all better" with her lovely Portuguese accent. When I looked down while breathing in to overcome the pain, I realized she had just gotten rid of the cyst in my hand. She taught me a valuable lesson that day—don't panic, just ask for help.

Remembering that lesson, I really began to call on my network of healers to help me overcome my pain. I hired friends in need of work to come over and work on me for pay. The expenses could have piled up even more quickly, but I still spent thousands just to get my shoulder back. I was lucky enough to be in a job where I could afford to compensate those friends for care, but they often would tell me, "No, this one is on me." I am immensely grateful to this day for their generosity.

A few years later when the pain had subsided, I was extremely tired of feeling off purpose, so I went on the hunt to get back into the work I loved and that enriched my soul and brought me a sense of fulfillment like no other work I had done. I cleared my head and thought carefully about what I would tell my patients to do if they came to me with the issue I was facing. I contacted a physical therapist and began a regime of strengthening with the goal of getting back into the work I love. I talked to an orthopedic surgeon and got cleared to go back to the work. Those were some of the happiest days of my life because I knew I would again be living my life purpose.

To this day, I continue to struggle with these injuries. I use the pain management techniques that I coach all my patients to use, and I find that if I moderate how much hands-on work I do, I can keep doing the work I love at a reduced level. Gone are the days of filling in for everyone or taking just one more patient even when my day is full. I set my limitations and I stick with them fiercely so I don't end up in the same situation again. I know I will not be able to do this work forever since someday I will be a very old woman with other health issues to face, so I savor every single opportunity I get to do my work, and I plan for the future when I will need to decrease my capacity even further.

> *Story Time:*
>
> *Jennifer Sheldon, LMP, shares her story with dealing with an injury, "I had a rollerblading accident where a cyclist caused me to fall and dislocate my elbow. I broke my radial head into about six pieces and destroyed three ligaments around my elbow. This resulted in surgery at Harborview by the orthopedic team. I had a titanium radial head put in, along with some screws, and had the three ligaments sutured around my elbow. My recovery process involved physical therapy three days a week for five months, receiving weekly massage and/or Reiki treatments, healing/Reiki circles, exercising regularly (within my limits), and focusing on my meditation and study of Buddhism, which eventually led to three months of counseling/therapy. I have regained a good portion of my range of motion; however, I still live in daily chronic pain. I am able to do a few massages a week, but I cannot get back to work yet.*
>
> *"The financial impact was devastating, to say the least. Having recently left my spouse, I was totally self-sufficient by working my two massage jobs along with my private practice. However, I was*

immediately unable to work. I drew on my savings and eventually received money from the sale of my condo. I was forced to accept many forms of help and healing from friends and angels in my life. I was forced to go to the food bank for about a month. I was unable to get any assistance, such as food stamps, due to visa/immigration factors. There were times I had to do what needed to be done to get by, such as selling my diamond earrings. I have not had any income for seven months now, but I am still getting by. I have a new plan that is in the process of being implemented. Financial challenges come up many times in our lives, but this one was particularly difficult because massage therapy was a new career for me that I absolutely LOVE, and my arm injury directly affected my ability to work.

"The emotional impact of my injury was shattering yet also healing in the end. It forced me to use my down time to look closely at many life events that had happened in the past year, and it forced me into repressed yet necessary modes—processing grief, loss, and PTSD. I fell into depression for a couple of months, which was scary as I lost my brother to suicide last year, due to depression. I went into a dark place, but I still spent 110 percent of any energy I had to focus solely on my healing. Therapy and Buddhism really helped me come to a place of acceptance and peace, and they helped me to know myself better than I ever have. Many people stepped up and lifted me up, by many means. I became a Reiki Master and was fortunate enough to have that gift during this trauma. It also changed my life and healed me on many levels; very powerful transitions are happening in my life and within my being. I see now that I am surrounded by so much love and that I am love. My path is now clear; I know my place in the world and where I want to be. I am now proud to call myself a wounded healer."

KEY LESSONS:

- Listen to your body before it is too late and you're out of work or doing a job you hate so you can get by.

- If you are injured, remember the impact your mood makes to those around you.

- Call on your friends for help to recover. Professional courtesy is to help our practitioner friends.

- Set limitations so you don't hurt yourself or burn out.

Chapter 10

COMMUNICATING NEEDS

Chapter Summary: Practicing setting good expectations will go a long way in prolonging your satisfaction with your career and your patients' satisfaction with you. Stay positive and be succinct in your requests. If you have a problem with your temper, get a grip on it before you let loose in front of a patient or peer.

THE BIG PROJECT TALK

When I began to write this book, I sat down with my partner and told her what we were up against as a couple. I set an extremely short timeline because I was challenging myself, and luckily for me, my partner is understanding about why I do things like this to myself. I told her, "I'm going to be working on my book quite a bit. I need you to tell me when I need to stop to take care of my relationship with you." Now, I don't have a family to answer to, but if I did, I would have included them in the conversation and made of them the same request. I am very fortunate to be able to say that my partner believes in me and is always 100 percent behind anything I commit to, which is a blessing. Your partner or your family may not be as receptive, but you can set expectations for the "big project" ahead of time, so you can meet your goals with more cooperation from others than if you had just started working on the goal without having a talk with the closest people in your life.

I also had a discussion with my business partner. Misty knew I was planning to change the way I approach my career and to take it to a new level. Because of this change in strategy, I let her know I wouldn't be meeting with her as much to create new patient acquisition strategies. Because I gave her the expectations that I would be working on a large project, she understood and chose to be my cheerleader. She understood I would be shifting my focus, and she switched gears to help me achieve the goal.

During the writing of this book, I took some days off at my partner's request to go recharge myself for writing more. We took a vacation to the beach to clear both our heads and spend time together. I encourage you to do the same if you are working on a large long-term project. Do not forget to take some time off so you do not burn out while you're doing this huge project. Your partner's request to have dinner with him or her or to go on a date of some kind is not an inconvenience—it is a valuable opportunity to get yourself recharged for your project. If you have kids and you're working on that huge project, make sure you pay the most attention to their needs because they are the ones who may have the most trouble understanding the demands you have placed upon yourself. If they have a recital or a sports event, go to the event and be there for them. Always be present when the people closest to you have indicated that they need you to be there for them. You will find time to finish your project as long as you budget your time. When these people ask you for your time, use the opportunity to break your chain of thoughts and recharge for your next wave of productivity.

CONVEY EXPECTATIONS CLEARLY

It's easy enough for me to say not to over-commit to anything so that you lose your balance in your life, but the truth is that such scenarios will present themselves over and over again in building a practice or any other large project you do. The important thing is to set expectations and let the people closest to you understand that you will be available at their request and be fully present for them when they request your time.

We must convey our expectations clearly in order to get our needs addressed. If I did not tell my partner how unavailable I would be during this project, I could have had a much bigger project on my hands than just composing this book—the project of rebuilding my relationship. Carefully setting expectations can take a great deal of finesse and skill, and it is something you should work on learning how to do your entire career and lifetime. You'll be setting expectations with your managers, your landlords, your family, your friends, and your patients for the rest of your life, so it should become a well-practiced habit.

The first hurdle to overcome is making sure that your expectations message is clearly understood. Follow these steps to make sure you're conveying your expectations well:

1. Clarify in your mind what your objective is. Get clear on what you want to be the outcome of this conversation.

2. Avoid being evasive or unclear on details. Be specific about what you expect. If you're talking about a specific project, give start and end dates. Being unclear can quickly lead to misunderstandings.

3. Be completely transparent about what you need. If you are unclear on what exactly you need, then you need to get clear on it before approaching someone to discuss it. Without this clarity, we may communicate a sense of frustration or confusion, which is not constructive.

4. Don't stress the negative—stay positive with your message. If you say, "Don't think about monkeys," then you start thinking about monkeys. By saying what we don't want, we often end up manifesting that very thing in the relationship—focus on what you want to see happen.

5. Ask for thoughts and feedback on what was said—hear out the person to whom you are making the request. Ask statements like, "How does this make you feel?" or "Can you tell me what you think I meant?" so you can get a closer understanding of how the request is being taken.

6. Ask with kindness—don't make demands. Sometimes it is helpful to be firm with someone, but asking is not about being firm—it is about asking long before you need to be firm so you avoid the need to be firm later. Make sure your request is not being interpreted as a demand. Ask yourself what will be the consequences if the recipient of your request decides not to do what you request, and make sure your response isn't emotional in nature. If so, you may be making a demand.

7. Try not to be too wordy in your request. Be succinct and short in your approach.

LEARN TO CONTROL YOUR TEMPER

I've seen many practices where practitioners take argumentative, emotional stances against conflicts with customers and peers. I have watched these practitioners lose customers by being inflexible and letting their emotions run rampant. Some of those practitioners burned bridges forever by not being able to control their tempers, and subsequently, they got bad reputations in their communities. Controlling your temper may seem like common sense to some of us, but for others, it is their Achilles heel. They may be the most amazing practitioners, but their impulsive reactions to tough situations leave damage traces in ways that cannot always be immediately seen.

Angela Guest, RN offers some good advice about the importance of professionalism in the health care field:

> As an RN, you're representing your company. A patient spouts off at you and you have to be nice. Doctors are our customers; patients are our customers. In my line of work, there are so many choices for patients to make. There are all these hospitals around here. People now are more informed. They choose to go to one hospital over another, based on not only their experiences but those of their friends and families.

Man seems to be capable of great virtues but not of small virtues; capable of defying his torturer but not of keeping his temper.
— Gilbert K. Chesterton

A nurse I know who often works in the operating room with surgeons constantly comes home with stories about unnecessary aggression she saw the doctors display. They have a fierce drive to get things done because lives are on the line, but in the process, they bulldoze their staff. She has a more stressful job because of them and hates her workplace because of it. People who work with her are looking elsewhere to work for the same reasons. These doctors are creating a hostile work environment and creating more cost for the business because of the turnover. It's expensive and time-consuming for businesses constantly to have to replace staff.

Work on your skills in this area if you feel you have moments when you may lose your temper at your office. Never let your stress get the best of you in front of your patients or other peers because it's a surefire way to have a story circulating about your problem with your temper throughout your town and in your professional community.

KEY LESSONS:

- Taking on a big project? Have a talk with the people who will be affected the most.

- Slow down. Think it out. Talk it out.

- If you have a problem with your temper, you had better fix it soon.

Part 3

MARKETING YOURSELF

Chapter 11

YOUR IMAGE

Chapter Summary: Make sure you always have a business card and your elevator speech polished before leaving the house! Get clear on what makes you happy by creating a mission statement, and then follow that feeling to discover your specialty.

YOU MUST HAVE A BUSINESS CARD

I think I've met at least a few people who didn't bring their business cards to their networking meetings. The reason why I say "I think" is because off the top of my head I can't remember who they were. My point is that you're a lot less memorable without your card. I try to make it a point to hand out at least five of my cards each business day. You want people to make a mental note of you and be reminded of you when they look at your card.

Some people have a unique style and flair to their business cards while other people just print out some cheap ones off their computers. I've seen successful people who use both methods. The important thing is that the card is readable and makes clear what your profession or specialty is. For example, when people use scanners, it can be difficult for the card information to be read if there is fancy writing on the card. I use an electronic scanner that is an application in my cell phone to automate organization of my cards, send LinkedIn invitations, and send introduction emails. By using this process, I think I must have saved a few small trees because I can email business cards when a referral is needed.

The best business cards, in my opinion, are the ones with your picture on them because then people will be more likely to recognize you the next time they see you. They'll keep putting the face to the name every time they look at your card. Also, I strongly recommend you include your email address on your card because people use email addresses to connect with you on social networking sites. If some information changes, get some new cards and try not to be handwriting loads of new contact information on all your cards—it makes you look transient in nature and offers a poor first impression that you are unprepared.

My business cards are so important to my networking efforts that I keep a box of them in my vehicle. Because I know I won't remember anyone who didn't give me his or her business card, I am pretty good about making sure I have cards before I leave the house. There are days when you're going to run out of cards; in those situations, if you have a moment, run to the local copy shop, or fire up your printer and run off a few copies if you can. It's good to have a spare template saved on your computer to print your business cards just in case you run out. Yes, they are that important.

ELEVATOR SPEECH (30 SECOND INTRO)

> *Cherish forever what makes you unique,*
> *'cuz you're really a yawn if it goes.*
> — Bette Midler

Most often the first thing that you'll do in any networking situation is introduce yourself. To introduce yourself well, you need to have a carefully crafted elevator pitch. At one open networking event, I was meeting all kinds of people. I had a newly minted elevator speech that was still being solidified in my delivery. A group of five people were around me, and one lady turned to me and said, "What is it that you do?" I flubbed up my elevator speech by replying, "I'm a massage therapist who works with people who have been in car accidents." She responded with, "Oh, that's so common." Obviously, I didn't make much of an impression on her by flubbing my carefully crafted intro, so I will probably never get a referral from her. However, her rude response also left me uninspired and unimpressed by her people skills, so I quickly forgot her name and what she did.

Remember, some people are just getting into networking and may need a break when they aren't as articulate or organized as more seasoned professionals. Recognize that these people may have a talent you don't know about so give them a chance by trying to draw them out of their shells to learn about their skills. Quickly dismissing someone as a "common" person is a very fast way to be viewed as a snob. That is the last way you want to be viewed at a networking event, so always work hard to be approachable and polite.

I consider my elevator speech to be an evolving tool, so I don't suggest you make one now and never change it. I do suggest that if you change it, you rehearse it over and over again until it floats off of your tongue effortlessly. To be completely honest, it's not that easy for me to give an effective one, so I have to work very hard at it.

Here are some examples of what to do with an elevator speech and what not to do:

Don't: I'm a massage therapist.

Do: I'm a massage therapist who specializes in treating neck pain.

Don't: I'm a health coach.

Do: I'm in the work of helping people achieve their health and wellness goals through coaching them on healthy behaviors.

Always keep your elevator speech or intro to thirty seconds or less—don't be a time hog. People are generally looked down upon when they ramble on about themselves, and it makes it harder for the listener to pick out exactly what it is that the person does.

FOCUS YOUR INTENTIONS—CREATE A MISSION STATEMENT

One way to focus your intention is to create a mission statement for yourself and one for your business. Mission statements are easy to remember statements that define your goals and your purpose. Taking the time to write down and to memorize your mission statement will help you to focus your intentions. If you advertise your mission statement to your customers, it may help them to identify you.

A mission statement isn't a document you file away after you've completed it, or that you pat yourself on the back for dreaming up, only never to look at it again. You need to keep it visible where you can see it on a regular basis. It will help you to keep "living on purpose." If you have employees, put it right on the employee manual where employees can't miss it—preferably on the cover. Include it in advertising—your brochures, business cards, and stationery. The point is always to have it right in front of you so you never lose sight of your purpose and the reason you started down the path you are on.

Here is one method you can use to create your mission statement:

1. Pick a central theme that ignites your spirit and resonates with you. Choose the purpose that appeals to your values for you, your employees, and your customers.

2. Make your statement an action statement. If it's just a statement, then it's not a mission statement—it's a marketing tagline. You want to make this statement say what you aim to fulfill every single day of your work.

3. Focus on key things about your purpose that resonate with you. Think hard about what you care about the most.

4. Don't make your statement in a quick and careless way. You'll have to look at it for a long time, and you don't want to have to sit down and do it over again frequently. Stay focused and on target once you've set your mission. Don't do—Ready, Fire, Aim. Always—Ready, Aim, Fire.

A personal mission statement is something I've used for years to focus where I'm headed in my life. Mine came to me one day in a class I took to create it at Landmark Education called the Forum. Here it is:

I strive to be a positive influence on every life I touch.

Some people will make multiple statements to reflect themselves, but I personally like just having this one.

BECOMING A SPECIALIST

> *Your profession is not what brings home your paycheck. Your profession is what you were put on earth to do with such passion and such intensity that it becomes spiritual in calling.*
> — *Vincent Van Gogh*

While you're visualizing your future, think about what you or your employees will individually be doing from day to day. Is it working with a specific type of patient? Or do you like to take anything that comes your way and be generalists?

When you become a specialist, you narrow the market at which you're targeting, and you're giving listening cues to your audience. When I put "Neck, Jaw, and Shoulder Specialist" out to the world, it was amazing how I had more people coming to me with the conditions I find the most joy in solving. While specializing can have its ups and downs, it actually makes it easier for other practitioners to realize your strengths and send you the right patients. You also have less people to compete against for patients because the majority of providers are generalists.

The best way to pick a specialty is to listen to your soul and not the numbers you could make. If you get really fired up about helping somebody in pain, then you should look into being a pain specialist—that is what I love to do. If you love working with people with a certain type of disease or problem, then focus all your training on becoming the absolute best person for solving that particular problem. The point is to resonate with your purpose and do what gets you fired up and excited about what you're doing—follow the happiness.

Specialists can also legitimately charge more for their services because they inherently have to have more training than generalists. You have to pay for the training to become a specialist somehow so it only makes sense to charge slightly more for your work once you have acquired the training and experience.

KEY LESSONS:

- You need to help people remember you, so always have a business card handy.

- Practice your Elevator Speech and keep it to less than thirty seconds.

- Focus on what makes you happy and follow it—doing so will lead you to your specialty.

Chapter 12

LOOKING FOR A PLACE TO PRACTICE

Chapter Summary: There are as many types of practice combinations as there are personalities to match them. Choose carefully where you practice and be picky—there's other fish in the sea. Working at home is not always what it's cut out to be in your head—investigate it thoroughly before doing it.

WEIGHING THE PROS AND CONS OF TYPES OF PRACTICE STRUCTURES

In the book *Starting a Medical Practice: The Physician's Handbook for Successful Practice Start-Up* by Kay B. Stanley and Jeffery Daigrepont, I learned something that simply blew me away. It made perfect sense really, but doctors have the same decisions to face in choosing and building a practice as pretty much every other health practitioner there is.

When you consider a solo practice, you're probably drawn in by the sense of independence, rights to make all the decisions, and the rewards you'll feel from finding things that work well. The problems most solo practitioners face can be the risks of practice mismanagement, the incredible task of finding patients/clients, and the problems that come with having no financial backup when things go wrong.

A small group practice can be an alluring proposition because you'll have the efforts and resources of others to combine with your own, while you'll still have a small establishment so you can take a larger role in making decisions. However, it can increase your problems in other ways such as being responsible for another person's performance, having less independence in making decisions, and a greater possibility for financial loss because of someone else's mistake. Even with the risks involved in operating a small group practice, I personally think it is a better position to be in than in solo practice.

With a large group practice, your immediate success possibilities are greatly magnified, but you lose a lot of autonomy in making decisions. The overhead and risk are spread greater because of the greater number of individuals. Some group practices are financially intertwined professionals, all with their own businesses underneath the umbrella of a larger organization.

Other times, the larger organization is an employer and holds all the staff under it as employees. These situations can create great referral opportunities to network within the clinic or hospital, which when done right, can catapult a newcomer to success in the office. The beauty of being an employee is well known with its low financial risk, its regular paychecks (although not always guaranteed in size), and the lack of involvement in the practice's administrative work. However, most people leave this type of arrangement because of the limitations for their growth potential, their lack of say in organizational decisions, and the instability of having their futures directly tied to the organization's proper management.

It takes a very strong willed person to be completely independent. It takes a real team player to do well in a group practice of any size. When we first graduate from our training, I think the best thing to do is to look for an entry-level, employee position in a group—that is what I would do if I could do it all over again. This first position will provide you with a lot of information that will be useful in the event that you choose to work for yourself, and it will give you the confidence to pursue it. You will also waste much less money when you start your business because of everything you have already learned.

INTERVIEWING FOR A SPACE OR POSITION

Success is not the key to happiness. Happiness is the key to success. If you love what you are doing, you will be successful.
— Herman Cain

Before applying for work or starting your business, feel out the area thoroughly. First, get some time on a local instructor's calendar to interview him or her. Start with the teachers, instructors, or coaches you know, and ask them who else you should talk to about the business or employment position. Take lots of notes—always appear intent to learn everything you can even if you feel the information provider isn't giving you much to go on. Little details about lessons learned can mean a lot. It's important to write down the experiences of others while you're interviewing them with the intention of capturing the smallest details. Some advice will be bad advice, so it is up to you to filter it out based on your observation skills. It helps to interview many people to create this filter. Go with what the majority says about the area first before taking one person's experience as gospel.

If you're looking to start your practice in any given area, call upon the people you know who are already in the area. If you don't know anyone, ask a teacher to introduce you to people in the area. Try to interview at least five people who are doing similar work to yours in that area; interview more if you can find them. When you quit finding out more new information, then you know you've interviewed enough people.

Whether you are being interviewed or interviewing someone else about the area, ask the following types of questions:

1. What is it like growing your business here?

2. Would you start a business here again if you knew all you did today?

3. What would you change about your practice if you had infinite resources?

4. What other practitioners are in the area?

5. Do you personally know the other practitioners in the area?

6. Is there anything you now wish you had known when you started your business?

7. If you're willing to share, what ways of marketing have you used that worked for you?

8. If you're willing to share, what ways of marketing have you used that did not work for you?

9. What types of services seem popular here?

10. What do you feel is the best way to encourage customer loyalty?

11. What is the crime rate like around here? Have you had any issues?

12. Have you heard about any other people's mistakes that I might learn from?

13. What would your single biggest piece of advice be for me starting out here?

14. What else should I think about before building a practice here?

Gathering lessons learned from others in this manner not only helps you understand the experiences they may have had, but it also builds rapport with other practitioners by showing them respect and that you value their information and experience. It's about creating that rapport with your neighbor, so don't assume the interview will be the end of your relationship. Nurture the relationship afterwards by staying in touch—I'll talk more about staying in touch a little later.

These questions aren't only helpful for someone looking to start a practice as a self-employed practitioner, but they can also be very useful as an employee. Don't think that just because an employer is going to market you, promises to fill your schedule, and alleviates the stress of marketing by doing it for you, that you don't need to know details like these. Just put a different spin on it by realizing that you are building the brand that is YOU. You're going to put a lot of effort into any place you work, and it's important it's the right place. Being an employee doesn't mean you're not building a practice just like a self-employed person would. It just means that it should be easier to find paying clients because someone has already done a lot of the work for you. Employers LOVE employees who are proactive about learning more about the business of practice building and will be impressed with you if you have taken the time to learn more about what it took to be successful. It will also give you a new appreciation for the work the employer had to do to build the practice.

I'm not going to tell you to dress nice and take a shower for your interview—you should have drilled that into your brain by now. When attending an interview of any kind, whether it is for a space or an employee/independent contractor role, just make sure you dress the part. That doesn't mean put on your best suit. As a business consultant at Microsoft and Intel, I quickly learned that the most successful folks weren't always the people who wore the super nice clothes—they were the ones with drive and people networking skills. In large organizations, you have to work very hard or network very hard to stand out, and you have to know the right people to get the right opportunities.

Dress yourself for what you want to attract—and decorate your space to do the same. If you want construction workers, find somewhere construction workers go and provide a shower at your office for when they get off work. If you want to attract the pierced and tattooed crowd, then by all means keep your piercings and tattoos and put your shop next to theirs. Just don't expect a potential employer always to be interested in the same market as you are.

> *Story Time:*
>
> *One chiropractic and massage clinic where I substituted was in a terrible location in a crime-ridden neighborhood. The clinic itself was run down, needed some paint, and a remodel. The massage room was coated with dust and cobwebs. I had the opportunity to work there longer, but I decided not to because of my allergies to dust and the headaches I left with every day I worked there. Astonishingly enough, the clinic was constantly busy with patients and barely had to advertise at all. Pay very close attention to the environment of a clinic to make sure there are no potential issues like this for you.*
>
> *Another example is a "mega clinic" that requests all its employees wear uniforms. The employees have scripts and checklists to follow for most of their daily duties. The new patients are given a video to watch. One patient described the experience of going to this clinic as feeling like she was going to a fast food restaurant. While this clinic is successful in its own right, it may have overdone its approach. This heavily formula-like, structured environment may work great for some people and especially new people to the health profession, but it may be a nightmare to others who prefer a laid back structure where they are free to inject more of their personality into their work.*

A good way to find out if you want to work somewhere is to visit the clinic as a "mystery shopper." Start off with this to-do list prior to applying for a position:

1. Feel out the clinic by calling the receptionist. Is she friendly and considerate? Does she sound uppity? Make conversation.

2. When's the soonest time you can get in for an appointment? If it's today or this week, expect that you won't always be busy there and the clinic is still in the process of building its practice to capacity.

3. What do the local or national review sites say about it? Look at the reviews and read them. Remember that some people have poor skills at setting expectations and may not be good communicators with customers. This flaw will show in their ratings.

4. Check the crime statistics for the practice's zip code. Simply go to "Google.com" and put in the keywords "crime statistics" along with the zip code.

5. Drive by or stop by the office location. What does the area look like?

6. Ask people you know whether they are familiar with the practice. What do they know about it? Do they know anyone who has worked there before? If so, find out if you can talk to that person and feel out the situation more. But when you go in for an interview, NEVER reveal that you talked to a previous employee or space renter because it can be detrimental to your chances of being hired if taken harshly by the prospective place.

7. Notice the attire and atmosphere of the location. Are the people wearing business casual? Do they wear uniforms? Uniforms say a lot about how rigidly a practice is run. Are the people well kept? Do the people have good energy?

8. Google the place online to find anything else you can about them. This can provide valuable information about

how the practice advertises and what kind of target market it works hard to reach. It can also provide clues as to how well the business is run.

9. Does the business have a website? What does it look like? Is it professional looking or amateurish? Is every page finished on the website? If it is unfinished, consider that the business may not feel the website is a good enough time investment or a top priority. If someone doesn't have a finished professional looking website, you can suspect that his or her methods may be lacking timeliness or being up-to-date. Everyone has reasons why he may not be keeping up with the latest trends, but simply having a great website is important—we live in the information age, so as a business, we have to provide as much information up front about how we operate in order to establish a trust relationship with our potential and existing customers.

10. Does the space resonate with you? Do the people's methods seem ethical to you? If they do not do treatment methods that you feel are legitimate, you should not work at that space. Imagine if you were working there and customers asked you about a treatment; would you be able to come across positively about it? You should always be able to speak well about the place you work and the other people in your group.

11. Do you like the way you were treated when the people working there thought you were a customer? Did you notice an unhappy customer there when you came in? If so, how was the staff handling the situation? For me, what worked was I would simply walk in and say hello. I'd tell

them I was just checking out the area. Be conversational unless the staff is extremely busy.

12. Take note if the office is extremely busy because if employees see a new person coming in their door, they should be welcoming and not too busy to talk.

13. Take note if no one is there to greet you when you come in—it could mean the office is low on funding and cannot afford someone to greet patients. Often, this situation is very frustrating for patients, especially older patients who like to have some personalized help along the way. Not having a greeter or receptionist doesn't immediately make it a bad place to practice; it may just be that the practice expects the employees or people who rent space there to do the work of a front desk person, or it expects you to hire your own help.

14. Finally, always thank the employees for their time after you've had a look around, and then go on your way.

When you're in an interview for a space or an employee position, make sure to ask any of the questions above that you didn't get answers to, such as whether you need to hire someone to greet people or answer phones, wear a uniform, etc. By coming prepared to an interview with questions and pen and paper in hand, it helps you to appear more proactive as an employee, which can enhance your chances of getting the job. Showing a desire to learn more about what it took for the practice to become successful shows that you respect the work the owners and employees have already put into the business, and the interviewers will respect you in turn for asking. Starting off your relationship with respect is important because even if you don't end up working in that area or for that person, you have developed a rapport with him or her.

> *Story Time:*
>
> *A therapist I met at a local networking event presented herself well and incited me to create a referral relationship with her. Her love was working with patients who were pregnant, and since I had an injury that prevented me from working well in the positions that pregnant patients required, I was initially willing to refer these patients to her. She had years of experience in her work and appeared to be a great referral partner from first glance. After the meeting, I learned her space was merely upstairs from where the meeting was held, so I asked her for a tour. She happily obliged and took me up a winding series of stairs to her office.*
>
> *At the top of the stairs, I took in the surrounding environment. The building was old and tired and the bathroom for her space was more of a utility room stationed about twenty feet from her office. The smells coming from the adjacent offices were pungent with the smell of art projects and other construction. When we walked into her space, I looked around at the furnishings. She had clearly been working on a very low budget. All the furniture appeared to be a bit worn and the strong stench of incense perfumed the room and choked my perfume allergic throat.*
>
> *I thought to myself, "Why would she want a space so high up when most pregnant patients would have trouble climbing all these stairs? Why would she perfume her space so heavily when most pregnant patients would have trouble with all the smells of the building, let alone her space's incense?" It occurred to me that this person hadn't thought through her location or her target*

> *audience. She could have considered a place on the first floor, away from the scents of the neighbors, and perhaps a place near somewhere that attracts maternity patients—perhaps a birth center, a maternity store, or a hospital.*
>
> *Finally, she needed to notice what she was doing to turn off the people who actually made it to the office. Her hands-on work might have been remarkable, but the strong scents and the environment could have made it unappealing for her clients to come back.*
>
> *I really wanted to provide feedback to her right then and there, but I could tell she took a lot of pride in the design of her space and I wanted to be polite. It's hard to tell someone you've just met when he or she has not done something quite right. Good coaches take time to get to know the person before they deliver feedback. If you run into a similar situation, I suggest you keep your opinion to yourself unless directly asked for it. Workspaces are usually a passionate practitioner's pride and joy. Just don't go there.*

Avoid these types of problems by asking yourself what your target audience wants by creating a focus group of people who could be your clients. You can interview them in a group or one by one. The valuable information you will gather from these focus groups or interviews will provide you with ideas for how you should shape your space.

Formulate questions of your own to ask, and include the following:

1. Does your target audience include patients who may not want to travel far?

2. Does your target audience need disabled parking nearby?

3. What kind of environment do your patients want to be in when they come for your work?

4. What things are they looking for in a practitioner?

5. What products/services would they like to see the most?

6. Are they likely to require a space without stairs and wheelchair access?

7. Do they need a bathroom nearby?

Getting clear on the target audience for yourself and figuring out the differences in each place you consider will save you much effort in the long run. Just because a location is cheap and available does not mean it will be right for you. You need to weigh carefully whether the location has a longstanding benefit for your personal career goals.

GET IT IN WRITING

A verbal contract isn't worth the paper it is written on.
— Sam Goldwyn

Whichever scenario of group practice or space rental you choose, get your offers and agreements in writing and every last detail on that contract before you sign it. Take a copy home and keep it in a very safe place. Contracts are often what can break a relationship in the end. Be very careful what you agree to because some people ask for things that may not be legal—I'd be wary of any practice that offers you an ethically questionable compensation plan. I've found it beneficial to ask that a copy of the contract be emailed to you before you go in for the interview.

Make very sure you're comfortable with the non-compete clause. If you live extremely close to the location, your non-compete could become a problem when you look for new work or start a practice at home. From what I've heard, not all non-competes hold up in court, but you don't want to take chances that hurt your likelihood to support yourself later in your career. While not competing with your employer is a matter of professional ethics, in the real world, non-compete problems happen somewhat frequently.

WORKING AT HOME

Working at home sounds great, and for some, it can be. But as I mentioned earlier, I've tried it, and I have decided not to repeat the experience. A lot of the problems with working at home seem to be invisible until you run into them.

Work-life balance tends to blur when you have a home office. When you're self-employed, you'll do a lot of your work at home anyway unless you sequester yourself in your office anytime you have work to do. I've met some therapists who do use an office to help them keep work at work and home at home.

When you contract with insurance companies, some of them will want to inspect the premises. Consider this fact when you have a household full of kids and pets making a mess every day. Also, consider that if you have pets, you will be excluding clients who are allergic. Clients can also unknowingly bring colds and contagious illnesses into the home when visiting, which puts at risk any residents of the home with suppressed immune systems. If you have an outbuilding, you are still allowing these people to know exactly where you live, so bringing strangers to your house must be comfortable to you unless you have an existing client base or are extremely selective about referrals. Often, the home atmosphere will encourage friends to dawdle or be very casual about the timing of their appointments, which can be a frustrating waste of your time so be prepared to handle these situations, or think twice about working from home. Not everyone is cut out for it.

> *Story Time:*
>
> *In the city where I live, I would have to pay for a neighborhood review committee to do a review on whether or not I could practice at my house because of the very strict zoning requirements. I would need to pay a $700 fee to get the process started. I decided not to pursue the possibility any further after another massage therapist told me of her experience in going before a review committee to get her home approved as a practice location. She was unsuccessful because of neighbors who were unhappy for all kinds of odd reasons such as increased traffic, even though she would add only approximately four cars to the street per day.*

BEING PICKY IS SMART

When choosing a space or a group practice, or whether to be an employee or self-employed, remember there are plenty of fish in the sea for your patients to choose from so you have to stand out. You need to be just as picky about choosing an employer as you are about choosing your own space to practice. Don't look at every interview opportunity as "the One"—just think of each one as a candidate. Consider a potential employer's motivations—the person interviewing you is going to make money off of you by providing your services or by renting to you.

Story Time:

When I was looking for new team members on one occasion, I had a stack of forty identical resumes from the advertisement I placed—all of them were recent graduates who must have taken a similar class on how to structure your resume. I had to go with my gut on which ones I would interview, and luckily for me, I chose a fantastic person out of that stack, Joleen Black, LMP. Her resume didn't stand out; I just went with a gut feeling that I should interview this person. Fortunately for me as her manager, I had just hired what I call a "Pied Piper"—someone who was amazingly successful with a little coaching. I had gotten lucky in hiring her since I didn't always have such luck finding good team members every time.

The same scenario can be looked at from the interviewee's perspective. When I was looking for work in the beginning of my career, I happened upon one place that would interview me even though I was very new to the profession. Its shop was new as of the month I interviewed there. The room to practice in was unfurnished, and I would need to build the practice with them. Something told me not to work there even though the staff was eager to have me on board. When I came back three months later, the shop had shut down already. Teaming up with a new shop is not always a good idea; clearly, I would have probably wasted a lot of time and effort on a place that didn't have the means to survive for the long haul. If you are going to be an employee or self-employed, either way, make sure the place you select has been around for a long time, has a good reputation, and is in an ideal location for the type of clients you want to attract.

KEY LESSONS:

- Carefully choose your options between solo, group, partnerships, or employee ventures based on your personality type. What environment suits you best?

- Always get all your agreements in writing.

- Be cautious of overbearing non-competes.

- You're always interviewing, whether you're renting or looking for a job.

- Working at home is not as cool as it ought to be.

- A lot of places are out there for you to practice—be picky about where you go.

Chapter 13

SELECTING A GROUP PRACTICE

Chapter Summary: Even if you're self-employed, you'll be interviewing when you go on the hunt for a space, so treat it like an interview. Be very picky about where you choose to put your practice building efforts so you avoid heartache later. Interview your landlord before you jump in because he may not have the same idea you do. Take a good look at the clientele of neighboring businesses to get an idea of the type of traffic your office will be near.

LOOKING TO RENT A GROUP SPACE

Let's say you want to be self-employed, and you are looking for a space in any given area. When you call on a space to view it, remember you are being interviewed then too. Some group practices will be extremely picky about whom they choose to work with; they may not tell you you're being interviewed, but they will look at the interaction that way.

When selecting a group practice, remember to feel out the person to make sure he or she isn't going to treat you as an employee even though you're paying rent. Unfortunately, this situation happens all too often. Some people don't want the complexities of paying employees, so they will instead rent a room and consciously or subconsciously hope to gain an employee in addition to the rental payments from the space. If someone asks you to give him a cut of your income in addition to space rent, politely decline the offer, but continue to gather information and build rapport. This person wants an employee more than he wants someone to rent space. He may frame the position as, "I'm looking to build a partnership and I need incentive to refer to you." This incentive type system has been used far too often and does a large disservice to the practitioner starting out. Also, this type of rebating for referrals can be illegal.

Group marketing can be a huge advantage if you're starting out. That means the phones are already ringing there and a lot of the legwork has been accomplished to get the ball rolling. It's a beautiful thing to walk into a practice that already has traffic, but it shouldn't be taken for granted. However, again...some groups may expect you to do something to keep the ball rolling, but they aren't necessarily up front about what exactly they expect. It's your responsibility to determine these expectations and not walk blindly in without knowing. It's also the establishment's responsibility to have a clear picture of what it expects you to do. It's important to clarify those expectations before starting out with any place.

Be wary of spaces that are too eager to have you. They may have turnover in their group for a reason. Think about it—the person renting the space wants to look as good as possible so you will pay him or her rent. Maybe his motivation is that you will help to pay the rent he has been struggling to pay. You need to be picky even if the other person is not. There are plenty of places for you to start your practice.

Interview questions for finding a group practice:

1. What do you expect of me as a person who rents here? (Community chores, group marketing, hours you keep, etc.)

2. Why did the last person move on from renting here? (If there was a person before you who moved out, remember you may not be told all the details about what happened.)

3. Do you have any requirements about referring to other practitioners in the group?

4. What types of marketing programs has your group done together in the past? What worked? What didn't?

5. What makes a successful practitioner here in your group?

6. Who in the group or nearby the office do you recommend I build a relationship with to start?

7. Do you require me to participate in marketing activities with the group?

8. What services seem popular within your group?

9. Is there anything else I should think about before starting out with your group?

One office where I interviewed wanted me to start out by paying a nominal rent, and then it would change to a percentage agreement when my practice had built up. In the end, I would have made a more decent living by staying with the rent payment, but the office wanted to make more money off of me being there so it formulated this plan. It wasn't necessarily a legal practice, let alone ethical, since I was going to be held responsible for building a practice as a renter, and then I would become an independent contractor after becoming successful, which seems backwards. The bottom line is to be very sure you're moving into a rental that is the right situation for you.

SET EXPECTATIONS IN GROUPS

When I first started out, no one was interested in hiring me since I was so new to the profession. My goal was to get the experience necessary for future opportunities, so I started my own practice in a small chiropractor's office. As I said earlier, the chiropractor offered me something I thought was unheard of—an extremely cheap small room to practice in his office. It was more like a closet since I could not walk all the way around the table, and my body mechanics suffered because of it.

In time, I noticed that I was busier getting people to come into see me than he was. The problem came about quickly that the chiropractor wanted me to send those people to him. Unfortunately, he had adjusted me once and set off a bad case of sciatica and I lost days of work because of it. Due to that experience, I had trouble referring people to him.

Over the course of the year at that office, the chiropractor seemed to grow more and more jealous of the traffic I was generating in the office. Just before the end of our relationship working together, he gave me a stern conversation about how he was disappointed that I was not sending referrals his way, so he wanted me to pay more rent. A short month after that, he told me that he would have to shut down his office and offered to let me take over the lease. I didn't have the means to do that, so I was forced to move out and lose all the work that had gone into building that practice.

What I should have done was set expectations with this chiropractor to understand that I would work hard to send qualified referrals to him. I should have learned everything I could about his methods from him and understood what he was trying to do. I also should have taught him all I could about what I was able to do. When my injury from his adjustment happened, I should have given him feedback that there was a problem instead of hiding it from him and considering his work problematic for me. I should have worked out this situation by helping him as a new doctor to understand what had happened for me. I could have been more successful there by helping him build his own practice and skills. I should have worked with him more on joint marketing efforts for the practice. These preemptive efforts may have saved that office from being closed so soon.

CHECK OUT THE CLIENTELE

Consider carefully the clientele at an office when you are viewing it. Who are the businesses nearby attracting to that area? Are they the type of people with whom you want to work? I once took a job in a city that was known for having ongoing issues with prostitution. During my time there, I was sexually harassed by clients more times than any other in my career. I should have taken a hint by accepting what I had heard from my mentors about working in that area and avoided it entirely.

Go to neighboring businesses close to the candidate location. Take a moment to have coffee in a nearby coffee shop, or to visit the local gym. Look around at what other health care practitioners are nearby; what types of clientele are they attracting? Pay attention to all the details the clients you would like to see would be looking for in a location.

> *Story Time:*
>
> *A massage therapist interviewed with me and absolutely sold her skills and background to me. I was so confident she was a fantastic pick for the practice. Before long, I figured out the error of my ways—I did not feel her out well enough. She clearly wanted the job, but she was very unhappy with the clientele that would frequent the practice. I learned from a patient that she had been making racist comments, and then I overheard some of them myself. In a clinic that was primarily patronized by people of one cultural descent, she had chosen to reveal her racist views about these people in the clinic to a patient and was subsequently fired. Was it mostly her mistake for applying to a clinic full of people she had formulated a stereotype about, or was it my fault for being the manager who brought her into a group she would ultimately hate? This situation has puzzled me for years as I've wondered how I could have prevented it, but honestly, I believe this person should have taken a good look at the clientele beforehand and asked herself whether she and her beliefs would make her a good fit in an ethnically diverse practice.*

KEY LESSONS:

- Be wary of rebating agreements with other professionals.
- Interview your potential landlord thoroughly.
- Watch carefully for the kinds of customers that nearby businesses attract.

Chapter 14

THE OFFER

Chapter Summary: Review any contracts or agreements thoroughly and don't sign anything until you have done so. Be clear on your compensation structure before accepting the job.

DON'T JUMP ON IT

Let's say a group practice picks you to rent its space or you decide to work for someone else. It's important to lay out all of your options in front of you, and to weigh the pros and cons of each option carefully. Choosing a job or practice location quickly and then quickly leaving it will tarnish your reputation and paint you as a flaky person. Also remember that the person hiring you is most likely going to make money on your presence at the clinic. You are part of the service team, which makes you a valuable commodity. Don't let it go to your head—but do keep in mind that you have a distinct monetary value to the person who hires you or rents you space.

If you're looking to be an employee or independent contractor, be wary of agreements that pay a percentage, agreements that limit your ability to move on after you work there, and low wages to start. Always get everything in writing when you start a position. Carefully review your contract for details that may come up as issues later. Established practices will often include a non-compete, and if you spend much of your time building a practice there, you will inevitably want to take your work with you. While there are many ethical issues surrounding taking patients with you from your former employer, the truth is that patients will do whatever they want to do, and you don't want to be sued for someone following you of their own free will. You also don't want to be penalized for keeping a relationship going after you've put in all that work with your patients.

Nor do you want to be fired for giving out your business cards to your own private location while working for someone else—this practice is very unethical if you do not have permission.

> *Story Time:*
>
> *A massage therapist wrote in confidentially, "Upon receiving a better offer, I was going to leave the practice. I gave my notice to my immediate manager who then told me, "Go ahead and let your patients know." However, he wasn't the owner of the clinic; he was only my immediate manager. I did take six patients with me, but unfortunately, the owner of the clinic thought I had taken many more in an underhanded attempt to take his business. I didn't think I was doing anything wrong by letting my clients know where I was going because my manager had appeared to give me permission to do so, but in the end, I was doing something wrong because I didn't really have the permission of the actual business to take the clientele I had built with me. If I had been on my own, and my patients found me by way of the Internet or my advertising after leaving, then the issue would be much less of a problem because they found me of their own accord."*

Let patients follow you by their own means—not as a result of you telling them all the details of your new space, but remember they will only follow you if you have made it possible for them to find you by making yourself visible through other means. Many people might have a bone to pick with a person accepting her former employer's clients, but the bottom line is to remember that people will do whatever they want to do—just don't steal patients.

EXAMINE YOUR OFFER

> *Story Time:*
>
> *I once received an amazing offer for work, which included all the things I wanted—a steady salary, health benefits, and paid transportation to and from work. I looked at the offer letter and thought, "WOW! I'll never beat that generous salary anywhere else!" After a year of being there, I realized I had made a terrible mistake—I didn't ask questions when accepting the offer to see whether the benefits they offered me were included in the gross amount for my salary, which they were. This made a $45,000 a year salary turn into $24,000 in my pocket after benefits.*

When you have any additional agreements in the offer, make sure they are well articulated and written down so there are no misunderstandings. Don't put off writing them down and making it a signed agreement or part of your revised contract if it's not included. Don't start the job before all agreements are fully understood and written. Review the contract three times to make sure you understand what you're agreeing to so there is less of a possibility of a lawsuit in your future. Misunderstandings are often the biggest source of pain for people, but they can be prevented by being very clear on mutual expectations.

> *Story Time:*
>
> One practitioner writes, "I was offered vacation time as a benefit for my position. I felt very fortunate to have received the offer, and I thought it was a sure thing that this vacation time would be paid out upon my leaving the company should that time ever arrive. It did arrive, and with an unpleasant surprise—I didn't get paid for that vacation. It was an offer the manager retracted upon taking it personally that I left the company. I never got it in writing and I lost needed money because of it."

LOW PAYING JOBS

> *Story Time:*
>
> A massage franchise chain made me an offer once. It seemed a bit low at points, but I thought it was pretty reasonable based on the income expectations the manager had set for me. I thought it would be just fine until I got the employee handbook in my hands and read the details of the compensation program which didn't quite sound like what I had just heard from the manager. Then I asked the manager how many sessions he was doing per day to achieve his success and he told me cheerfully, "Ten." Most therapists would know that is considered a bit much.

Be cautious of entering into employment in these types of situations, especially if you are setting boundaries about your limitations and they are not being honored. Agreeing to work for a low price can hurt your profession as a whole by making the whole profession appear to be able to accept a substandard wage.

For example, if you agree to give away chair massage as part of your employment agreement, you have just discounted your chair massage to zero. Now when someone thinks of you, he may consider your services are free for chair massage since you didn't put a price on it. If you have to give something away, make sure proudly to display its regular price. Sampling is an extremely effective way to help consumers understand what you do; just make sure they don't think it's always going to be free.

If you put a small value upon yourself, rest assured that the world will not raise your price.

— Anonymous

Please keep in mind that large establishments cost money when you are offered a lower wage than you expected, but they take the most tasks off your plate like answering the phones, paying the rent, doing marketing campaigns, or providing supplies and equipment. The lowest overhead establishments often create the largest returns but often ask the most of their practitioners.

Story Time:

A very experienced therapist applied to our office, and I was very excited to meet her. We listed the wage agreement on the job posting and were very clear on our terms for the position. She came in promptly and we went to a private place in the office to chat. I could tell she was tense, but I dismissed it as interview anxiety. The situation quickly went bad when I realized she had came in merely to belittle me about the wage at our clinic, and as she began to yell, it just escalated even more without me even talking. The problem was that I couldn't control the wage, but I could

> *control who we hired, and since this person just wanted to argue with me about something out of my control, I showed her the door.*
>
> *I never wanted to offer a wage that wasn't acceptable to some people, but as a manager, I had to think in terms of how many tasks I was taking away from the position at hand if that person were on her own. When the compensation was designed, many things were taken into consideration—like the level of the people we planned to hire. When we were able to get a very experienced person to accept the lower rate, it was a win for the organization even if I wanted to give the practitioner much more. The practice needed to achieve certain goals to stay viable. Of course, I always wanted to give my whole team a huge raise, but after learning the overhead of running an establishment like that, I knew we couldn't do much better. It was the business owner's responsibility to choose where the money was going and how much was going, and as a manager, it was my responsibility to present it to potential new employees as the rate we offer. It's hard for some completely to comprehend, but until you run a business, you will never understand the burden of overhead and the importance of a business emergency slush fund.*

On the other side of the equation, the more people who accept low wages, the more patients will think they can pay little for services, the more the insurance companies will feel they can pay us less and less because our "market rate" has dropped, the more our professions are cheapened over time, and the more the perceived value of our services is diminished. Do the math and make sure it's a living wage for you specifically before even considering applying if possible—and don't listen to the hype about how much you "could" make by working there. Do the math for yourself before you get a financial rude awakening.

LEAVE ON A POSITIVE NOTE

It can be very difficult to nail down the perfect place to work since everyone is on his or her best behavior when you arrive for your interview. I've made many mistakes along the way in trying to save relationships, but I've ended up turning those situations into learning experiences. I can clearly remember some situations in my past where I totally blew it and I know it. Nobody is perfect, but whatever you do, try to leave a good impression with whomever you interact, even if the person is ridiculous. You never know when you might need someone's help later or run into him or her at an event.

When you choose a place to work, think hard first about what inspires you before choosing something that will just pay the bills. Then focus on going after those places that are a good match for your personality type. For example, one massage therapist I interviewed told me she was tired of the repetitive nature of doing spa type work. When we moved onto the practical, I quickly noticed that she seemed to have lost her injury treatment skills. I decided not to hire her because she wasn't going to fit the needs of the job at hand. If you're starting out, choose your employers wisely—don't just choose a place because it will get you a lot of experience. Make sure it is the right experience for the direction you want to take your career. If you need to redirect your career midway, make sure to polish up any old skills before trying to move onto the next career. Had the massage therapist I interviewed polished up her injury treatment skills, I might have hired her. In other words, don't leave a substandard impression if you can help it.

It is one thing to be unqualified for the work you're applying to and know you are unqualified, but it's entirely another to think you're qualified and not be. I'm not saying you shouldn't aim high, but I am saying to be realistic about your capabilities and apply for what you can handle. A person who is horribly underqualified for a position wastes the time of the person interviewing him or her and can leave that impression of being underqualified in the interviewer's head for a long time afterwards. You don't want people in the community to think your technique is substandard. Be up front and honest about your skill level.

Take your interactions and interviews very seriously—you are leaving a lasting impression about yourself in these situations. The health community is amazingly small, and people will remember the impression you left on them. If you're active in the community, you will run into people you may love to see and probably at least a few you'd rather not.

> *Story Time:*
>
> *I once interviewed a therapist to provide hot stones massage. She brought in all her equipment and appeared very legit, so I allowed her to perform a practical on me. After the practical, I had burns and scrapes up and down my back. Needless to say, she didn't get the job. She clearly needed to refine her skills prior to applying for the job. Some years later, I ran into this person at a conference—every moment I was speaking to her, the indelible mark left on my mind was the memory of those hot stones.*

KEY LESSONS:

- Don't just accept any offer.

- Examine any contracts carefully and get all additional agreements in writing.

- In every interaction and the interview, always leave a positive mark on the people you interact with because you never know when you'll run into them again.

Chapter 15

EVERYBODY'S AN ENTREPRENEUR

Chapter Summary: When your employer asks you to market the practice, accept it as an opportunity to market yourself and the brand you are. Sometimes it takes awhile before you can be on your own full-time. Be patient and don't quit your day job until you're good and ready.

PROMOTE THE BRAND THAT IS YOU

> *The major value in life is not what you get.*
> *The major value is what you become.*
> — Jim Rohn

When you start out in the work of being a healer, you may go to work for someone else and quickly dismiss that you're not an entrepreneur. The problem is that you're very wrong to make this assumption quickly. Everyone is in sales, no matter his or her profession in health care, and everyone is building his or her own practice. Period.

An employee may come on board and hope that a bunch of clients will be happily handed to her so she will be busy forever and ever. Unfortunately, this is a bad assumption. I haven't met an employer yet who not only expects you to bring some clients in with you by marketing yourself, even though you work for him and he promised to do the marketing, but who also expects you to retain the current clients he has. You can't just go to work, provide services, collect your paycheck, and go home. It won't last long doing it that way, and you will have done yourself a great disservice by not doing some self-promotion.

> *Story Time:*
>
> *One therapist I hired had some of the most amazing hands I had ever experienced. I thought for sure she would be a huge success at our office, so I happily hired her after she agreed to participate in marketing the practice. We had a booth in a busy mall nearby that allowed an opportunity for our therapists to do one marketing event per week by providing chair massage demos at this booth as their contribution to making the practice grow. One day, I peeked in on the therapist at the booth from afar—as a supervisor should do when having employees sent out into the field alone. She didn't have the chair to do chair massage. The therapist looked like she was carrying a ball and chain to the booth. Her posture reflected that she hated what she was doing. She was unapproachable and unprepared. Her lack of interest for what I thought would be a sure success for the practice quickly showed the problems she had with self-promotion.*

As a health care provider, you may move from practice to practice in your career for a wide variety of reasons. Wherever you are working, you'll find that the most important brand to promote is YOU. When employers ask you to help market the practice, step back and realize they expect you to promote yourself and not just the practice. It's about drawing more business in and using the power of a team to create business.

GOING OUT ON YOUR OWN

Many people like to dream of owning their own businesses. Many other people don't feel like they are fit for owning a business so they never go for it. Many people who go for it unfortunately fail because they didn't do some part of their business right. Plenty of people appear successful to everyone else, but they are really flat broke and in debt up to their eyeballs. Then there is the top minority—the people who are wildly successful and have so much abundance that it would make anybody's head spin.

Most successful people have had to try incredibly hard and be uncommonly persistent. I say uncommonly persistent because that is the truth—there are a lot of people who need to call upon more resources, mentors, and coaches to help them become successful. Until they learn how to be persistent, bull-doggedly running after their goals by having someone get behind them and push them along the way, they may never be successful in the practice they have.

Kate Phillips, Wealth Coach, jokes about budget realities in her article, "The 'Are You Ready to be an Entrepreneur?' Test." She instructs us to:

> Add up the costs of a professional branding, marketing and website, legal advice, coaching and consulting, all business licenses, insurance, and certifications, all equipment and clothing, continuing education and office rent for the first six months in business. Now, double it for good measure. Add on the basic living expenses you will need while your

business ramps up. This is the amount you need to start your business. Now, divide it by 25. This is your budget. Good luck!

The important takeaway is this—don't just start a business without some help. First things first, don't quit your day job because that is part of the help that will make you successful. It's critical that you have some stability in your life while you adjust to having part of your income be unpredictable. Of course, most people are just waiting to burst out of the gates just like at a horse race. Think of the tortoise and the hare instead—take your time getting your ducks in a row for your business. Most people I know in health care often have two locations or more where they are employed while practicing becoming self-employed—in other words more than one source of income. Call on your resources, hire a coach, and don't rush yourself into a large debt in the process of going full-time into owning your own business.

> *Story Time:*
>
> *I knew a massage therapist who was starting his own practice at a location nearby the chiropractic office where he was working and the management took note. He was watched considerably by the management to see whether he was taking advantage of the situation and was often left out of opportunities because he decided to open his office in such a close proximity so they looked at him as "competition." Sure enough, he was eventually fired because they found out he was using their outreach programs for his own practice promotion. Don't ever advertise your own practice while working for someone else unless you have his or her explicit permission.*

Choosing to go full-time will often be the hardest step of them all. You will soon see while running your newborn business that the ups and downs are numerous. People you thought you could rely upon may not show up, and customers you thought would pay sometimes don't. It's a harsh reality to learn, but you can soften the blow by having lots of seed money put aside. Many people recommend six months of seed money for living expenses on top of whatever expenses it will take to keep your business running.

The first thing you want to do is run through your mind what it will be like to be self-employed with a fully open mind to the possibilities. I've heard being self-employed referred to as "financial sky diving," which I think is a perfect description. Self-employment is not all as rosy as many like to make it sound. There are serious ups and downs in income patterns that happen when starting an office and while running it over the-long term.

There is also a monstrous time commitment to doing self-employment right. It's not a part-time job—in all of my experience, I've found it is two full-time jobs. I often say to my friends, "I work sixteen hours a day so I don't have to work eight for somebody else."

KEY LESSONS:

- You are your brand—even when working for someone else.

- Choose to be cheerful about marketing for someone else—it's not that bad of a deal.

- Use care when going full-time and keep your day job as long as you need to.

Part 4

NETWORKING LIKE YOU MEAN IT

Chapter 16

WHY I DON'T ADVERTISE

Chapter Summary: The best way to get clients and patients in your door is by trusted word-of-mouth. By far, it's the best technique for building a practice sustainably, but this technique takes time and effort to make a lasting effect. You may end up with a love-hate relationship with your review sites as they pump up word-of-mouth. Serve the greater good when you're marketing and reap the rewards of being noticed.

WORD-OF-MOUTH

When I was twelve, my father sat me down, gave me a fatherly talk, and told me he was going to teach me responsibility. We weren't a wealthy family, so I somewhat understand why he felt the need to do so. He told me I would have to start paying for my portion of the various things I used around the house, and to buy my own clothes, pay for my food, and contribute to the household expenses. Looking back, I can see the problems with asking someone to do all of that at twelve, but at the time, I took it on—it was what I was supposed to do because Dad said so. I know now this request was wrong of him, but in my current day-to-day life, I have an odd sense of gratitude for this loss of my childhood because it taught me a lot.

Unsure how I was going to help with the household expenses, I went to my church pastor to ask him for help on what I should do. When he said, "Why don't you watch our cat and our dog while we're gone on vacation?" I happily agreed to do so. Upon his return, he handed me the biggest check I'd ever received to that date: $220. The next Sunday at church, the pastor said to the congregation, "I just want to thank little Jodene Hager for watching our pets while we were on vacation. She did such a great job." I was approached by a bunch of people at the end of the service who wanted to give me more business. Word spread so quickly that soon I had a thriving pet sitting business that helped me contribute to my family. Before long, I found myself hiding $100 bills in the light sockets around my house to keep my parents from knowing exactly how much I was making. To this day, I doubt they have any idea exactly how well I did in my little side job.

This experience taught me a valuable lesson about word-of-mouth. The congregation trusted the pastor with their faith, so naturally they would trust him to give a good recommendation. With a congregation of over one hundred people, about ten people approached me after the service. That one referral generated ten times the amount a mailer would have done. A little known fact about mailings is that if you do a mailing to a group of one hundred people, the mailing will be considered successful if you get one or two people who respond—that's a 1-2 percent response rate to be considered successful. My response rate was much higher at 10 percent just from one word-of-mouth recommendation.

Building a business without an advertising budget is completely possible and I've seen the most successful businesses do it. A one-doctor chiropractic office with a small team of massage therapists was one of the busiest offices I have ever seen, even though the clinic was dusty, old, in a bad part of town, and in need of a serious makeover. In contrast, a giant chiropractic clinic that poured tens of thousands of dollars every year into having a professional marketing coordinator, advertising, leasing a nice space in an affluent part of the city, and having its rooms all decorated by professional interior designers was growing at the same rate as the small practice.

Why was this small practice so busy? It was because of word-of-mouth and a team effort toward the most important goal—productivity. The most compelling part of its success strategy was the focus by the front desk team members to call patients to remind them if they forgot to schedule an appointment so any holes in the schedule would be filled; they also kept a waiting list on the side just in case something opened up. The big office with all the money invested in advertising and image never had a waiting list, so clearly it was not working for them and they should have focused their attention on the things that worked best instead. The small office was focusing on what was most important to keep the business running, the whole office productive, achieving its weekly goals, and only using the methods that worked best to keep those goals attainable.

Dr. Gary Silverman, who serves arthritis patients in Arizona, states:

> I have been told solo practice is a dinosaur awaiting a meteor strike. In fact, we are currently closed to new patients. While

you might think how is that good marketing, for the last few years we were accepting patients only by referral. It creates the practice you want rather than sometimes off the street inappropriate referrals. I was recently listed in *Phoenix Magazine*'s top docs two years in a row.

Erin Presseau, Strategic Interactive Manager of Silvertech, a marketing firm focused on online strategies, said about generating word-of-mouth:

> First make sure you have something worth talking about. Listen carefully to find out what consumers consider important. For example, we worked with an organization that was promoting a new physician practice. They marketed the physician's credentials, the beautiful new office building, location, free parking, etc. But after listening in on Facebook posts, it quickly became clear to them that what got consumers excited was the extended office hours and low wait times. Once you know what gets them excited, ask your consumers to help you promote that specific aspect. So in this example, rather than asking them to spread that word that there is a new office in town, you will get better results asking them to spread the word about how long they waited to be seen at their last appointment or ask them to challenge their friends on who waited the least amount of time at their last appointment. Either way, planting ideas of how to share the information they are most excited about—often in a narrow and focused way—often gets the most success.

Ever notice how few individual doctors advertise their practices? Usually, it's the hospital they are contracted with that promotes the brand of the hospital, but no promotion usually happens for any specific doctor. Most of the business the doctors receive is primarily from referrals. Chris Morton, MD, said about the reason why doctors don't advertise, "It just doesn't give you a sense of confidence in that person because people don't pick out doctors the way they pick out a mattress. A commercial saying 'Big Bob's says he's got great prices' doesn't translate into the kind of thing people look for in a doctor."

Dr. Joseph Simon of Manhattan Physical Therapy and Pain Center says, "The most important thing I learned is that you have to make the prospective client trust you. So by giving out free information and advice without expecting anything in return in the short run, and creating that relationship and nurturing it, you will help create a follower and promoter of your practice."

When Misty Nault, MSA, L.Ac., and I started NW Pain Relief, we had a very small advertising budget. We had no radio ads, no newspaper ads, or other forms of advertising. We focused our efforts solely on networking groups; now, referrals are our primary source of new patients. Some people would be concerned starting out without a big advertising budget. We knew that if we concentrated on what worked best, we could keep our expenses extremely low and we have.

What works best is word-of-mouth—not an ad in the yellow pages, a full page ad in the newspaper, a coupon on Valentine's Day, or any social media marketing strategy. Referrals directly from other health care practitioners who have positioned me as a person they trust are the source of the majority of my patients. The best thing of all about word-of-mouth is it's free. Large companies often run gigantic marketing campaigns that intimidate the small businesses around them; however, running a strategic word-of-mouth campaign can produce even greater results than most traditional campaigns.

Social Networking online is not the end all of networking. It does not work exceptionally well to establish new client relationships, but in my experience, it does help to nurture existing ones. Many of my clients love to message me this way and to keep the conversation going long after the session has ended. We have a lot of fun with it, and I often run trivia contests to get new people from my social media fans to come into the office by giving away gift certificates. This enticement is the most successful method I have used yet on my site—not advertising specials, not talking about special events—just making the fans get excited about winning something. In conclusion, I have had some success in getting clients to come in based on getting to know me online, but I cannot say by any means that this is the only way you should do your networking. Far from it, you need to be meeting people face-to-face if you want to network to get the best results.

> *Story Time:*
>
> *Dr. Kevin Doner, MD, a Hematologist and Medical Oncologist, says about how he built his practice with referrals, "I'm a specialist (Hematologist/Medical Oncologist) so for me, marketing is important for a couple of reasons. I have to depend mainly on referrals from other doctors, primary care doctors, surgeons, etc., and it took me a few years out of practice to figure out how to approach this. For my particular specialty, we do market to the public, but that is less helpful I feel.*

> *I have been out in private practice nearly six years. I have been in two practice settings which both required different approaches. My first job was in a multi-specialty group, so I had a built-in base for referrals, and dozens of docs all in the same building/hospital. I was able to be very passive and just introduce myself, eat lunch in the doctors' lounge, etc., and do okay. I found that, when I got my first referral from another doc, it helped to call the person personally and chat and be accessible and communicate well.*
>
> *I left that group after two years and had to reboot my practice—in the same hospital, but I had to start from scratch with all new referring doctors. It took me a while to get going, but what I finally did was research all the doctors in the area via the Internet and local medical society and just take half to one day a week to make rounds on my own. By going office to office, dropping off cards, giving out my cell phone, etc., my practice exploded. Docs got to meet me face-to-face and connect and feel comfortable that I was a 'nice guy' they'd want to send patients too. Every year, there is an influx of new doctors out of training or who just move to town—I also make sure to target them early, introduce myself, and try to make a good first impression. Often those initial impressions and bonds you make last a career. Medicine still remains a very personal business between doctors, so as a specialist I have found this still to be a very effective way to start or build a practice."*

A recommendation from a fellow health practitioner generates buzz for you. The patient becomes curious and intrigued by you, and ultimately, usually checks you out somehow. Most often with a strong recommendation, people will actually visit you and give you an opportunity to win their business. A strong recommendation helps to justify your price and makes it more likely you will collect your full fee instead of providing a discounted session offer.

The keys to generating buzz about yourself are:

- Be memorable—do it differently than everyone else, with your own style and flair. Just make sure to run it past your mentors or coach first for constructive feedback. Asking for input on how you're being memorable can be a way to generate buzz too by letting the people know that you implemented their piece of advice. They'll feel a sense of ownership, and create a stronger bond with you, and then they have an investment in seeing you succeed.

- Provide a quality service that is unsurpassed by others—become the best of the best and work hard to stay that way. Call upon your mentors again to gather ideas of how you can build yourself up to be something worth talking about.

- Give people fuel for their talking—don't just expect that a simple normal patient encounter is going to do this. Find a way to be unique in your approach with something that appeals to people. Little touches of detail go a long way toward becoming unique.

- Ask your clients and fellow health care practitioners to spread the word. You will not generate a lot of buzz unless you do this critical step! You may never receive unless you ask!

- Stay in contact with your network with valuable interactions and acknowledge people who help you. Many business people get a business card and then add that person to their newsletter and believe that this is their way of staying in touch. Instead, it becomes impersonal, and eventually, most people will unsubscribe. Work to create face-to-face meetings, lunch dates, or coffee dates with people with whom you want to create a relationship. For that client you haven't seen in awhile, pick up the phone and say hello to see how he or she is doing. Don't make the call with the agenda to fill a spot in your schedule—let that happen naturally. Dropping a handwritten thank you card in the mail for a client or a referral partner for something of value he did for you can go a long way. Make the interactions meaningful every time—don't SPAM your connections.

REVIEW SITES

During my career, I've placed myself on business review sites along the way because it was a free way to get exposure, and I have gotten several clients from using this method. However, I consider this method a slightly risky way to advertise because once you place your information on a review site, it is now public domain and you may never be able to get it removed. Odds are that nine out of ten people will probably love me, but the problem comes with that one person who came with other expectations and was unsatisfied. When these clients mention these review sites as their source of referral, I often cringe a moment because I am extra on my toes from fear of making a mistake and getting a bad review from them. Also, a stranger who has never been to your office can post a random terrible review that can be very problematic to get removed—this situation once happened to me. Statistics say that the average unhappy person tells eight people about his experience, and these review sites have taken this scale to the extreme.

> *Story Time:*
>
> *One business I knew had a problem with a campaign its marketing coordinator had planned. The problem was that the campaign appeared to people to be a bait and switch when really the business was doing all it could to be forthright about its methods. The review sites quickly racked up tons of bad reviews just because of this campaign. The owner wanted very much to return his good name to normal, but because the review sites are using information in the public domain, he was ultimately unsuccessful. He may never know the full impact on his business of the one mistake of running that campaign that caused all those bad reviews.*

The right thing to do if a review site has damaged your reputation is either to hire a solid reputation management firm to clean up the mess, or to start responding to every complaint and work to resolve the situation with each one of the bad reviewers. While in some cases, the reviewer is unlikely to change his opinion, it reflects well on your business to show you attempted to make good of the situation. Most sites have a way to respond to reviews. Make sure you understand the review site system thoroughly before signing your business up for free publicity.

PROS AND CONS OF TYPES OF ADVERTISING

Many health care professionals around me have tried advertising only to find it quickly saps away their budgets. For that reason, I choose not to do any type of paid advertising anymore. The following is a breakdown of types of advertising, their pros, and their cons. These figures will vary, but they are typical of costs I have seen.

TYPE	COST	PROS	CONS
Word-of-Mouth	FREE!	Establish yourself as a trusted person because most often your referral partner has already established trust with the individual. Often you will get your full price for your services.	Time-consuming to network and create solid referral relationships.
Business Website	Varies widely, but can be free.	Can provide a great first impression and be a constant online source of advertising for web passersby.	Time-consuming and can be completely invisible if not promoted using other means and if not listed in search engines.
Online Unpaid Campaigns (Review sites)	Free to list yourself in their directories.	Get a lot of exposure to potential people if you have a lot of recommendations to make yourself noticeable.	The directory listing becomes public domain, and you cannot usually ever have it removed if something goes bad in your reviews.
Online Paid Campaigns	$0.70 per click to $1,000 or more per month for aggressive ad campaigns.	Using some venues such as Facebook, you can zero in on your audience. This method can be low cost and can have an immediate impact.	Smaller audiences, usually demographically vast, and audiences may ignore the ads. 80 percent of all online advertising can fail to reach the specific audience intended.

TYPE	COST	PROS	CONS
Billboards	$5,000 on up with art costs included—usually a contract of several months.	High repeat exposure as passersby see the billboard and your brand is etched in their minds. Lower competition from other businesses by using this method.	No ability to select your demographic, hard to track impact.
Print Magazines	Often between $1,200 to $5,000 per issue depending on the ad's size.	Demographic selection is easier based on the type of magazine. Often achieve credibility and prestige with the audience. Magazines are often passed along among people.	Long lead time and no guarantee of position in magazine (unless you pay for it); may reach too far outside your area to have a strong impact.
Radio	Starting around $15—$100 per advertisement. Bigger reach by the radio station demands a higher price.	You can be selective about the area you reach and the demographics of the listeners.	Auditory only; some people just don't listen to radio ads. Quick exposure.
Direct Mail	Roughly $1-5 per piece for postage and stationery.	You can be very selective where you send your advertisement and it allows personalization.	Time-consuming and can create a "junk mail" look to your business. Low response rates, and cost quickly adds up.

TYPE	COST	PROS	CONS
Television	Starts at around $500 per ad spot, but can find lower prices on rare occasions.	Mass market coverage, low costs per actual exposure, and combines sight and sound.	Can be extremely expensive, too many other competing messages, and less ability to focus on a specific demographic.
Newspapers	Depending on the size of the newspaper, can be around $100-$1,000 per week for a small ad.	Good local area coverage if you choose a local paper.	Short run times and most people don't pass along a newspaper like they do a magazine.
Volume Coupon Promotions (Groupon, Living Social, Fresh Guide, UrbanDealight, etc.)	Promotion company can take 30-50 percent of your price after you have discounted it already by 50 percent.	Lots of exposure to people who are looking to try your services.	Coupon seekers who often look for a special but do not come back until there is another special. Very low income from special.
Yellow Pages (Print)	Usually requires a contract for a long-term commitment and starts around $50 per month.	Gives the appearance of a strong solid business with a low cost and can reach newcomers to the area.	Not easy to cancel contracts of this nature. Outdated method since most people are going online. Make sure any contracts include online advertising.

All this is not to say that I have never advertised before. Quite the contrary—I have worked myself to the bone with the results of advertising. One practice where I rented space did a large volume deal campaign with Groupon. While it was an enormous success with bringing tons of new people in the door, it created a distinct problem with every therapist in the group participating—burnout. We were working our tails off for a mere $20 per session. Not only was this rate unsustainable, but the conversion rate into long-term customers of these coupon-seeking people was extremely low. This experience has led me to the conclusion that while getting that kind of visibility and traffic through your door is helpful in getting word-of-mouth going, it also trains people to wait until you have a deeply discounted special price instead of coming in for a full price treatment. You end up with a file drawer full of one-time visitors who were coupon seekers. It is up to you to give them strong reason to come back after that first visit, but when you're burned out, you may not be giving anyone a reason to come back.

For any of these advertising methods listed above, you should have a website to be your online sales representative 24/7. A website is something you must have now—don't delay. Long gone are the days of not having one or having a cruddy one. Make sure it's a user-friendly, professional looking website. You can outsource your website development to reduce cost, but I cannot say that all my experiences were perfect when I have done so. There are language barriers and virtual freelancers can have quirks. See www.hcprn.org for suggestions of vendors and sites to hire freelancers. Whatever you do, get very clear on what you want before contacting them. Mary Aske, digital marketing expert for the automotive industry, suggests, "Review websites that are well known. The formats of the websites are very dynamic. It doesn't have to be busy, but you have to go to the most successful websites. They've spent millions of dollars in usability studies, and this is what you've got to study about them."

At one point, I somehow found a way to work myself into a free booth at a local woman-focused trade show. I gave chair massage after chair massage away for tips, and I offered people a free half-hour session on my table with the ability to upgrade to an hour for a discount. I found this campaign to be one of my most successful because it cost me nothing but my time, and it did produce some repeat clients. My burnout level with this method was significantly lower than most other methods, and it didn't hurt my budget at all.

Greg Pursley, DC of PC Coaching says, "Marketing is constant and never-ending. As a chiropractor, I typically have to do more marketing than a traditional physician. I have learned that face-to-face marketing is most effective. Going out into the public and meeting people is best."

SERVE THE GREATER GOOD

> *If you desire to add value by serving others, you will become a better leader.*
> — John C. Maxwell, *The 21 Irrefutable Laws of Leadership*

The Massage Therapy Foundation once gave me a wonderful opportunity to build its social media campaign. How did I get this opportunity? It was because I asked the foundation how I could help. These volunteer experiences carry on in my career now and give me a network of unique resources—accomplished people within the massage community—to call upon. Simply being a volunteer for an organization like the Massage Therapy Foundation shows you are proactive and have leadership qualities. Exercise your capabilities and gain valuable insight while meeting peers in your community who may be some of the most dynamic individuals you'll ever meet. You will find that if you contribute a fraction of your time to the greater good of your profession, you will get much more back in return.

Working toward the greater good is the best cause of all in which to invest your leadership skills. Megan Holub recommends in her book *How to Make $100,000 as a Massage Therapist*, "You can check out the rating of any non-profit organization at www.charitynavigator.org. Their ratings will reveal to you how efficient and organized your charity of choice is, how much the charity's CEO is keeping as salary each year, and what portion of your donation goes to the cause versus the marketing costs."

In the book *Coaching Questions: A Coach's Guide to Powerful Asking Skills* by Tony Stolzfus, some great questions are provided as a good way to sort out what is really the particular mark you want to make in the world. If you can't hire a coach, I suggest you take a moment to read Stolzfus' thoughts on the legacy you want to leave behind and how the world will be a better place because you lived.

Choose your charity with your passion behind it and you'll find yourself in a win-win situation. It's incredibly rewarding to find a cause you are completely passionate about and choose that as your higher purpose. In my life, I haven't always been focused on my purpose and it has been a struggle. It seems to wax and wane from time to time when I have hills and valleys in my career. When you really feel you've found a cause into which you can invest all your passion, then it is like magnetic North in the compass of your soul.

> *Story Time:*
>
> *A chiropractic, massage, and acupuncture office found a local charity that needs donations of items for a local shelter. A couple of times a year, the office offers its services for free in return for donations to this shelter. The chiropractors give adjustments and new patient exams, the massage therapists give complimentary chair massage, and the acupuncturists deliver community acupuncture during the event. By promoting the cause, the office gets well-earned visibility for being a benefactor.*

KEY LESSONS:

- Word-of-mouth is possibly the most powerful lead-generation tool of all.
- Review sites are a double-edged sword—be proactive in their management.
- Serve the greater good and get noticed.

Chapter 17

BUILDING RELATIONSHIPS

Chapter Summary: To achieve any success, you must be respectful to others simply because they are human beings even if you have to earn their respect. Work hard to be approachable and clear your negative energy before walking into a networking meeting. Always follow up and maintain the relationship after you've made the connection. Find ways to keep in touch, and follow through on your promises.

BEING APPROACHABLE

If you want to build a solid relationship with someone else, the bottom line is you had better not meet him or her when you're in an off mood. When you attend networking events, you need to be an approachable individual who is ready and willing to meet new people.

> *Story Time:*
>
> *When I was starting out in massage school, I had an amazing teacher, Janis Lynne, LMP, who had a wealth of experience in the field. She did something unique that no other teacher did—"Dork Dancing." We students would come into the room with a*

> *ton of bricks on our shoulders from our daily lives, which would keep us from being focused on the task at hand—learning our new trade of massage.*
>
> *I remember the routine well—we would come in and drop off our books and supplies. Then somebody would run over to the stereo and put on some good dancing music. We would all get up and move around like we just didn't care, being as silly as possible, getting low into our hips, and moving around. Not only did this activity break our chain of thought, make us laugh, and get us loosened up for practicing techniques, but it also activates a different part of the brain for kinesthetic learning—which most hands-on healers are prone to be.*
>
> *I still use this brilliant technique to this day. When I'm lost in thought and just about to go into a meeting, I'll crank up the radio, dance in my car until it's shaking, and laugh at the person in the car behind me who thinks I'm crazy. This technique breaks up my stress, changes my energy, and gets me fired up about hanging out with other people.*

Dr. Stefan Black, DC, is amazingly appreciated by his patients, loved by the other staff in his office, and probably one of the most approachable people I know. He has found that by practicing a laughing technique before going into a networking meeting, he can change his energy so he is more approachable, no matter what stress he is currently facing in his personal or professional life. This technique can be found taught by Yoga masters and is sometimes referred to as Laughter Yoga. Laughter indeed is good medicine for your own soul because it will soothe that stress ball of energy we can accumulate during the day.

Misty Nault, MSA, L.Ac. is quite possibly the most approachable acupuncturist I have ever met. She has an air about her that entices people who are afraid of needles to give her work a chance. She often expresses that she loves people who are new to acupuncture, and she invites newcomers to acupuncture to come to see her because she will happily educate them about her work. On the other hand, I have met many acupuncturists who never explain what they are doing, quickly analyze a patient, treat the patient, and then move onto the next—all the while skipping the most important step of building a relationship of trust.

> *Story Time:*
>
> *I once visited a chiropractor from whom I was considering renting office space. He was jittery, lacked eye contact, looked uncomfortable in his chair, and was a general all around negative Nellie about his world. Before we could really get into details, I realized I would not be interested in renting space from this individual. His arms were crossed and he wiggled in his chair frequently as if he were uncomfortable. His anxiety was contagious and made me feel uncomfortable when I normally feel quite confident checking out a potential space. Not only that, but I will probably never send a patient his way because he acted so strange that day.*
>
> *What this chiropractor could have done was something completely simple—smile. If he had allowed me to see a genuinely relaxed smile, not a forced smile, I would have felt more warmth. He could have maintained eye contact with me while talking to me and used open body language that would tell me he was intent upon listening, not fidgeting, such as by having his arms relaxed instead of crossed.*

FOLLOWING THROUGH

In almost all avenues of our lives, we must learn to be trustworthy so we can develop solid relationships with others, and in health care, we must magnify our trustworthiness to the extreme. People trust us with their greatest asset—their health. If we lose their trust, we will inevitably lose their business.

In the workplace, we must balance being personal and being professional, and it can be a difficult balance to maintain when you are in a health care setting. Often, discussions with other health care professionals about what our own body is doing become prevalent and things of a very personal nature are revealed. However, when talked about carefully, you can use these topics to find common ground with another practitioner. Perhaps the practitioner has a hidden strength that could help your problem. All the while, be careful what you reveal about your personal health. Something said in confidence should stay in confidence, but often these conversations can become public—make sure to preface that you are saying something in confidence. Chat and be open with people; just be sure to be clear you're being personal when you are. Most, but not all, practitioners understand what confidentiality means.

Follow through is the most important aspect of relationship building. Follow through action is almost always best when done in person or over the phone. Sending an email can work marvelously too, but nothing builds a relationship like one-on-one real time conversation. I use my computer to track my calendar carefully, making sure I have at least one in-person meeting a week with my network to develop a deeper relationship with that individual. Using online tools like LinkedIn, I keep track of my professional network and go through my list of people often to make a list of those I haven't spoke to recently; then I follow up with each person individually—not with a mass email.

RESPECTFULNESS AND BURNING BRIDGES

> *Story Time:*
>
> *A Therapist writes, "While substituting at a clinic, I worked under a chiropractor who had a different opinion of how much knowledge I should have as a massage therapist compared to the doctors I had built rapport with in the past. Those doctors in the past knew me and knew what I was capable of doing for their patients. This particular doctor hadn't known me for very long. A patient came in who was seeing us because he had been in a nasty bar fight. He had pinched a nerve in his neck and was in considerable pain. The patient was sent to me for a massage prior to an adjustment one day. During the session, I palpated what felt like a large obvious tear in his trapezius. Not really knowing for sure whether it was a tear since I'm not a doctor and cannot diagnose, but knowing I should bring it up to the doctor, I attempted to convey what was going on with the patient before he went for his adjustment. The doctor half-listened to me, walked away while I was talking to him, and used a very dismissive tone with me, simply saying, "Yeah." I could not understand why he wasn't at least going to hear my opinion of what I thought I might have felt. Needless to say, I lost a lot of respect for him that day."*

When working to build relationships with others in your community and with your patients, remember you're building your network one person at a time. Make every interaction count and don't dismiss someone. Always approach people from a place of kindness. If you are too busy to talk, be considerate and let the person know that now isn't a great time to chat; then suggest another time. By giving the person another opportunity for your one-on-one attention, you are building your relationship so it will be a stronger and more solid one.

Some professionals may feel they are too good to network with professionals of other types. An owner of a physical therapy clinic once shared with me his angst about his physical therapy team, "I want them to get out and network with other people and not just the Medical Doctors with which they have their primary referral relationship, but they just won't move past that so they can build referral relationships with other types of professionals. It's frustrating to me because it holds back the success of the business. Also, these Physical Therapists know that they are in great demand, so it is very difficult to ask them to do something outside their comfort zone because they know they can just pick up and go work somewhere else."

Building a strong network with a variety of professionals pays off in many different ways. Once you have built these networks, you have a vast array of opportunities that can come your way, but if you change your connection by taking on a negative tone, you will quickly find that you burn more bridges than just the one between you and the one person with whom you thought you were burning a bridge. Often, people will think they just affected one person with a negative action, but they don't take into account the impact that one person can have on the rest of their network. One person will likely share a bad experience with someone at least eight times.

So many people come out of school or spend the better part of their careers wanting to hire a fleet of employees underneath them, all dutifully carrying out their duties, to bring positive change to the world around them in volume with the efforts of this dream team. I, too, was once in that place, but now I often get asked why I don't have a huge clinic. Most people really understand why I'm not too keen on having a big clinic anymore after hearing the following story.

> *Story Time:*
>
> *An employee I had years ago remains to this day the reason I am wary of hiring employees. She interviewed like a champ and made an excellent first impression, so I hired her right away, and I watched her quickly become a favorite at our office. She was cheerful and fun to be around, and I quickly settled into complacency as a manager, thinking she was doing a great job and having a great time. Then I started getting reports from the rest of the team that she had decided she wasn't fond of my management style and liked to gossip frequently with the other team members about negative things going on in the business. These reports made me curious because she always seemed to be so cheerful and fun loving when I met up with her.*
>
> *Then an insurance company came up with a question about a chart that was filled out but not billed. Unfortunately, I uncovered that she was filling out paperwork far in advance before her patients came in so she could leave for home sooner, which disappointed me considerably. When I came in to confront her, I walked in on her badmouthing me to my manager. Being caught red-handed, she got four inches from my face and yelled at me about what a terrible manager I was before she stormed out the door. I didn't even have a chance actually to tell her she was fired.*

Shortly after that, she had her partner call to tell the management that I had done something terribly wrong, and she wanted to see me fired. This action backfired on her because it was quickly seen as retaliation; she lost the respect of the staff who heard about the underhanded technique. About a week passed, and then something else strange started to happen. I had strange men calling my house and asking for very odd sexual things from me. I was scared and concerned for the safety of my partner and myself. Our phone rang around the clock with these callers. One caller stopped long enough to tell me where he had found my information; then he quickly hung up when he realized he was part of a vicious prank on me. I ended up having to go to a very unhelpful police station that could do nothing to protect me since I could not prove who had done the prank. The website that had posted the ad for the disgruntled ex-employee was unhelpful as well since it said it couldn't help beyond just removing the advertisement. The next strange thing that happened was people started slowing down as they drove past my house and looking at it. It was one car after another, after another. Perhaps it was paranoia building up in me, but I learned from that one caller who would talk to me that my name, my phone, and my address were being given out. I eventually changed my phone number and moved out of that house all because of this one employee.

The lesson I learned from this situation is that some people will at first present a wildly different face than the true face they have. It takes a long time really to get to know someone and to understand his or her quirks. In a professional atmosphere, it can be even harder to get to know someone since a person may be just putting on a face for work. Even when you think you know someone at

> *work, you probably don't know him or her all that well. Not only did this therapist ruin a relationship with me, but she also lost the respect of her coworkers and the business.*

After that experience, I now take my time building all of my professional relationships, and I consider potential employees more carefully than ever. I want to know them really well first. I want to make sure I can very confidently tell my clients that this person is ethical, balanced, established, and is going to take good care of them. I visit other practitioners' offices before I send a referral, and if possible, I let the practitioners demonstrate their techniques on me. It's a way of validating their success stories, learning to trust their expertise, and getting to know another health care practitioner on a deeper level.

KEY LESSONS:

- Respect others even if you haven't earned their respect yet.
- Use techniques to make yourself more approachable before going to networking events.
- Follow through on your promises and keep in touch.
- Network with all kinds of health professionals—not just your primary referral sources.
- Build bridges—don't burn them.

Chapter 18

COLLABORATION NOT COMPETITION

Chapter Summary: Even the most successful people have always had help, so don't get it into your head that you have to do everything by yourself. Get over the thought that people in the same profession or who provide the same service as you are your competition. There are differences between you, and you can build a bridge with them. Build partnerships with others to increase the chances of your success, but be very selective of whom you choose to partner with based on their strengths matching to your weaknesses. Find out what your potential partner needs and address those needs to strike a deal to promote each other.

NOBODY SUCCEEDS COMPLETELY ALONE

No individual has sufficient experience, education, native ability, and knowledge to insure the accumulation of great fortune, without the cooperation of other people.
— Napoleon Hill

There was a practitioner who had trouble keeping staff due to an assortment of issues in the business management of his practice. When these staff members would leave, the practitioner often burned the bridge with the employee by taking the exit personally, and an adversarial relationship would result even when the staff member felt he or she had left on good terms. One ex-staff member revealed to me, "I just don't understand why after all that time we built a good relationship that now we have to be unable to refer to each other." In time, this practitioner lost many referral partners from other practitioners by not focusing on keeping those relationships alive and healthy with professional respect even though the ex-employee had moved on to further his own career with a new opportunity.

Salena Rushton, Sales Manager for Context International, says, "Anything that is so exclusive of others joining in, it's a force of life, it's proven—it dies. Closed organizations die." If you ever have employees, do not make the mistake of making an enemy out of a potential ally. If someone leaves your office on good terms, keep those good terms alive with a healthy respect for the person trying to better his own life by moving on to the next big thing for him. Even if you are disappointed that someone is leaving your team, that person could potentially become someone with whom you really wish you had maintained a relationship. The person could have been your greatest ally in a marketing campaign you haven't dreamed up yet. The point is—never, ever burn bridges.

In the book, *Radical Collaboration: Five Essential Skills to Overcome Defensiveness and Build Successful Relationships*, the authors, James W. Tamm and Ronald J. Luyet, state, "Today nobody succeeds alone. If you don't have the skills to build relationships, you'd better win the lotto, because you'll never thrive in any organization, and you probably won't even survive in most businesses."

THEY AREN'T YOUR COMPETITION

> *Every Adversity has the seed of an equivalent or greater benefit.*
> — Napoleon Hill and W. Stone, *Success Through a Positive Mental Attitude*

Okay. Now's the time to get over it. The person across the street who seems to appear to do the exact same thing you do isn't your competition. Yes, I said that. No matter how funny it sounds—he really isn't. You have a unique offering from what he does and you are a completely different venue. There are plenty of customers for everyone to help—nobody is stealing your customers.

Some massage practitioners will blame the big spa that just went in next door for the failure of their business, as some doctors may blame the big hospital that just went in down the street. It's not the spa next door that caused the failure or the new big hospital; it's the mindset that "That new business went in so now we will go out of business" that caused the failure. Most patients are loyal and will stay at a place where they feel well taken care of even if there seems to be a sweeter offer next door to try them out. If you don't have customer loyalty, then you have another problem entirely.

Turn that situation around and you have something new to think about. You don't provide any spa services, but you have clients who like them occasionally when they aren't getting therapeutic treatments. What if you were an insurance provider and the spa across the way didn't have one insurance provider in its office? Perhaps you can make friends with the spa manager and work out a mutual referral relationship. Perhaps the manager would let you put your cards somewhere in the spa's office for the staff to give to patients in need of ongoing insurance-based therapeutic treatment, and perhaps in return you could put spa coupons out on your desk for your patients to see.

A strange "Us vs. Them" mentality exists between many professions that is completely unnecessary and counterproductive. I've seen chiropractors fear sending their patients to massage therapists, hypnotherapists cautious of what they say around counselors, and plenty of allopathic professionals hesitant to send people to alternative medicine.

If we only knew what each other was good at, accepted that it may be a technique we personally wouldn't feel comfortable using, and stored away the treatment method in our brain to keep for a later date, then we would be getting a lot more patients helped faster than ever. The truth is that when a patient experiences being healed, he is experiencing his own reality, which is far more valuable than any research can consistently prove. Contradicting data doesn't mean that it doesn't work for some people. It's about finding what works for each patient—orthodox method or not, it just has to be the solution that is tailored specifically for that patient's needs.

BUILDING PARTNERSHIPS

> *The enthusiasm for partnering is rooted in a down-to-earth fact: You're much more likely to succeed in a business with a partner than without one.*
> — David Gage, *The Partnership Charter: How to Start Out Right*

What none of us can accomplish on our own, we can achieve by working together. Now when I talk about partnerships, I'm talking about limited projects with a start and an end, such as a workshop or joint marketing venture. In some cases, the traditional co-mingling of risk and cost is a beneficial partnership—my main recommendation is that you do lots of homework before getting into this type of agreement. Friendships can be destroyed and dreams can fall apart when poor expectations are set in these types of arrangements.

The problem is that so many health care professionals who could be allies don't even talk to each other, let alone even consider collaborating together. Many of us sit in our practices all day, all alone, in our little self-imposed and isolated worlds, while trying to figure out our next way to reach the public and get people to try us, when we could have all the help we need to promote by promoting each other.

If you pull together health care providers from the same area, you'll find there are no two people who are alike and doing the exact same thing—when you do find two who are alike, let me know because I haven't seen it yet. Everyone has his or her own style, own niche, and own way of service delivery within his or her practice. Building partnerships with your fellow practitioners of all kinds helps pool your strengths, combine your capabilities, overcome your lingering divisions, and begin to develop an extremely powerful strategy to move forward for your mutual success. You give and you'll get—that is true in our world of practice building.

Consider it this way in an extremely simplified scenario. Let's say you own an ice cream cone shop and your only flavor is vanilla bean. A customer comes to you who says he doesn't like vanilla and was hoping you had something else. Instead of just saying, "Sorry, I don't have that flavor," you, being your helpful self, refer the customer to the ice cream shop across the street where he can find the chocolate fudge swirl he really wanted. That's not turning business away; it's helping out the customer. The customer remembers how helpful you are and may one day be in the mood for vanilla bean, and if you've built rapport enough with your neighboring ice cream shop, the staff there will remember that you have that awesome vanilla bean ice cream and send a customer your way who is looking for that. This scenario may seem idyllic, but it is completely possible to build a relationship of respect between two similar businesses, and I have seen it done again and again.

People in the corporate business world do this all the time—it's called peer networks. Many major corporations in the business world realize that relationship building and leadership development play a huge role in meeting goals. For this reason, many companies have sunk great deals of cash and time into developing networks to share best practices, passing on lessons learned, fostering our next leaders, building bridges to each other, and creating common visions.

INTERVIEWING A POTENTIAL PARTNER— TRUST YOUR GUT

Choosing referral or business partners is not something to be taken lightly or on a whim. The best thing you can do to attempt to make the right choice when partnering with someone else is to listen to your inner voice. Does it tell you that this person resonates with your purpose? Does it speak to you that you are supposed to work with this person?

Most healers are people with amazing healing gifts, but they have very little business sense. In rare situations, a person has a balanced combination of both. Sometimes, you can lean on your partner to bridge these gaps. When it comes to work ethic, this may be the biggest obstacle for anyone trying to create a partnership because it is the difference that breaks them up the most in my experience. When one person feels he is carrying all the weight of the agreement, he often feels it is an unfair arrangement and will bow out sooner, thus wasting valuable energy and possibly burning a bridge with the other practitioner.

It's important to feel out your potential partner through recommendations from another colleague, looking at review sites, asking people who have worked with him, checking out his credentials, looking for recommendations, and just listening to what your first impression says. If you get a bad feeling about something, listen to it, and wait for a better situation to come up before approaching the partnership topic.

It's good to present smaller opportunities first to a potential partner to learn what he or she may be like to work with. Best is to start with getting a demo from the person about his work and vice versa. You must be well-versed "fans" of each other's work and personalities because you may spend more time with your business partner than your spouse. You can't tell people great things about your partner if you don't know anything about what she can do or is like. Just talking about what you do with someone is not enough; give the person a full example of what you do from start to finish.

> *Story Time:*
>
> *A doctor writes, "I've made the mistake before of jumping into a partnership without really examining what caused the person to need a partner anyway. After being in the partnership for a while, I noticed that I was feeling like I carried most of the weight of the work and my partner was not trying nearly as hard as I felt I was. This created a sense of resentment, and no matter how much I tried to talk to the person about it, I found I just couldn't articulate what was going on in my head from fear of a confrontation; thus, I wasted a lot of time when we could have been constructively coaching each other toward a common goal. In time, I worked on my communication skills and found a way to draw this person out, get over my resentment, and create a successful business partnership, but if I hadn't checked myself it might have ended badly."*

HEALING GIFTS VS. BUSINESS MINDS

Most healers I have met are great healers, but often, they are awful business people. It may be managing their business or employees that will bring out an ugly side, or the mismanagement of their funds and records, or the lack of a proactive sense to take their destiny by the reins.

It's possible to make a business work without being successful at healing and business. Some of the most successful healers I know are the ones who decided to hire a coach to help fill in their lack of business sense. These people are helped along the way to make new habits that will enable their success.

However, some people don't even know that coaches exist, or they refuse to get help, so they flounder while figuring things out the hard way. That is not to say that every coach is worth the money and perfect for the job in your industry, but a good coach is like a "Band-Aid" you can apply to a hole in your skills.

Another way can be to lean on your mentors to add to your business skills. Sometimes even mentors may not have all the answers so you will need consultants. When you choose to bring on a consultant, make sure to interview that person the same way you would interview a coach—see "Chapter Four: Picking a Coach." Always remember, pay for experience, not information you can get by yourself.

THE "WHAT'S IN IT FOR THEM?" RULE

> *If you give, you begin to live.*
> — Dave Matthews

At the time I was writing this book, the Massage Therapy Foundation was doing its RISE campaign to raise money to benefit the foundation; its campaign tagline was "How will you RISE?" Since I was already feeling inspired with putting together my book release party, I decided that I would RISE by creating a benefit event for the foundation. It was amazing how at suddenly every turn I found a new opportunity to create a beneficial partnership to promote the event and get the word out. Every day, I was creating new partnerships with others to get something out of being there and being part of the event. Sponsors were stepping forward and offering out of the benevolence of their hearts. And as word about my book spread like wildfire, not only did it push me forward on my extremely tight deadline of twenty-seven days in which I challenged myself to write this book, all while running my practices, the networking groups, and balancing my personal life, but it increased interest and support in the Massage Therapy Foundation's benefit. My world became a whirlwind of inspirational action after action. I was a little delirious from lack of sleep, but the world felt like it was my oyster—so I ran with it.

Once I found the best venue in town for holding a big event, I asked the staff there whether we could bring a big audience to their facility for a charity benefit. The venue was then happily donated for the cause and the staff worked with me to create the best experience possible. When I asked the Massage Therapy Foundation to help promote the event, it got the word out and helped it become a success. When we worked to create sponsorships for the event, businesses stepped out of the woodwork to help out. When I needed friends to step forward and help hand out flyers, they happily did it for the cause. Not only did Health Care Professionals Referral Networking get an opportunity to have an amazing networking event, but the Massage Therapy Foundation had a fundraiser and got a lot of medical professionals to know more about it.

If you want to get, you must give freely and without expectation. There is a freeing sense of giving of your heart that creates a fire inside of your creativity. Besides the benefit event itself, several other people stepped forward to help raise donations for the Massage Therapy Foundation at this time. Here are a few more examples:

- A great instructor, Scott Wilson, LMP, stepped forward to perform study groups for the Northwest LMP

Support Group to raise donations for the Massage Therapy Foundation. He gladly gave his time to help out the students. This generosity also helped to promote the Northwest LMP Support Group's goals of having students fully prepared and aware of the support they have from the very beginning of their career.

- To assist the study groups, my business partner, Misty Nault, MSA, L.Ac., agreed to talk to the students by giving a presentation on Oriental Medicine because the licensing exams usually have on them a lot of questions about this subject area. As a result, Misty got to meet a bunch of new massage therapists who could someday be her new referral partners.

- For the Health Care Professionals Referral Networking, my friend Dr. Stefan Black, DC graciously offered a meeting room close to his office in a nearby mall for meetings. In return, he got to meet more people and draw more attention to his office by being the host. Instantly, that group experienced growth because of the need for practitioners to network in that area. We created another win-win.

When creating partnerships, whether to benefit yourself, others, an organization or charity, or your own business, follow the "What's in it for them?" rule. Look for what your potential partner needs and find out how you can provide it to him or her. The venue for the benefit for the Massage Therapy Foundation needed a big draw of people, so I promised to promote it. The Massage Therapy Foundation needed a fundraiser, so I created it.

It's all about making that first move. Focus your intention on the goal and benefits of a partnership and make the first move. You'll find as you do it more frequently that you get better and better at starting and organizing something and engaging the right people to get it done.

When trying to create a charity event, start with these steps to create winning partnerships:

1. What is the greater good that your efforts can help? Focus on what matters to you and your profession the most first, but then look to medical research charities to raise your cause. It is better for your business to be a side note to the greater good task at hand. Promoting your work as a benefit for a higher cause incites others to give out of generosity and not just to give you their business.

2. Find a great partner. Look for someone who is going to complement your work style or needs. The person should have something you need, and you should have something he or she needs. Get it clear in your head what you will be providing for the person and what he or she will be providing for you. Be 100 percent sure about the person or establishment with whom you're partnering.

3. Approach people from a business proposition; tell them what you can provide—don't oversell them. Just be excited about the opportunity. It doesn't take a lot to sell a win-win. Use email sparingly; save these conversations for in person, or over the phone. It's best to discover win-wins when someone can hear the excitement in your voice.

Hearing the excitement ignites your potential partner's excitement.

4. If you will co-mingle funding in any way, keep vigorous track of the finances and get agreements on paper. It's best not to co-mingle funding at all. If you must pay for anything at any point in the partnership, always get the agreement on paper.

NW Pain Relief was born out of a partnership as well. Misty Nault, MSA, L.Ac. was someone I admired for her acupuncture skills and her social butterfly magnetism. I felt we could complement each other's work styles and refer patients to each other because of the differences in our work. We learned to promote each other's work while keeping our business finances separate. We split costs to make the entire business more affordable for both of us. We brought our various items needed to run a clinic and put them together, removing the burden of just one person having to purchase all the necessary items. It was another win-win.

When picking a business partner for a joint venture, keep these steps in mind:

1. Get very clear if this is the correct business partner for you. Not everyone works well in a team, and it's important to realize early on whether your business partner has a tendency to be lazy. Try very hard to get a business partner who is just as much, if not more of a go-getter than you are.

2. If you're jointly going to promote a single business, work together to establish expectations of what that means to

both of you. What will each of you do to work toward the greater benefit of the business?

3. Write down any joint agreements for expenses and get clear on what is expected of each partner.

4. Pool each other's strengths. Find out what you each really like to do best and run with it. Work hard to figure out what works for each of you.

PARTNERING TO PROMOTE EACH OTHER

> *When no one worries about who will receive credit, far more can be accomplished in any group activity.*
> — John Wooden, author of *They Call Me Coach*

An easy partnership to form between like providers is a partnership based on location. A local chiropractic office I know of rented a trade show booth and then split the cost between multiple chiropractors in the area who were out of the range of their office. That way when someone came up to the booth at the trade show, a different chiropractor could man the booth each time so it was always staffed. When the chiropractor found a new potential patient after a short screening, the chiropractor would then give the person the corresponding business card to an office in the area where the patient would like to be seen. The people were given options to choose from multiple doctors based on a location that worked best for them. One key takeaway learned from this method is that people want to stay close to their home or their work. When you pay for a trade show booth yourself, make sure it's pretty close to your office because the people coming to the show will most likely be primarily local.

Story Time:

In the large group practice where I managed the two massage departments, we had to build referral partnerships and trust just the same as anywhere else—the major difference was that we worked together constantly. Our mutual success was great for the business, but instead of working toward what benefited the business, we worked to make each other successful as individuals because we worked together as a team to make it happen.

We started out by using simple networking techniques. Massage therapists would introduce the chiropractors to their techniques by offering demos and the chiropractors would provide care to the massage therapists and explain their work while providing it. At the beginning of each therapist shift, the massage therapist would come to the chiropractor and let him know what openings she had for the day and the chiropractor would work hard to fill the openings with pre-qualified people who needed massage. Once the massage therapist was presented with the opportunity, then it was up to her to ask the patient whether he wished to reschedule following the session. From there on, the massage therapist worked to establish a relationship of trust with the patient just as the chiropractor had done prior to the referral. Likewise the relationship went the other way when a patient came in for massage only. The massage therapist would learn from the chiropractors how to screen a patient for chiropractic and introduce the patient to a chiropractor after his massage session if the patient chose to do so.

All the office staff members were introduced to each doctor and practitioner's method with free treatments, which the office staff loved. It was great to see the team bonding and becoming cohesive in time. Friends for life were made at that practice.

KEY LESSONS:

- Successful people almost never achieve their success all by themselves.

- Your neighbor who does the same thing as you is not the same and thus not your competition.

- Be a partnership builder—but choose your partners wisely.

- When creating partnerships, always follow the "What's In It for Them?" rule

Chapter 19

NETWORKING GROUPS

Chapter Summary: Realize that networking is an essential part of your career and that your career can suffer if you don't do it. Learn to go to networking events to socialize, not close the deal. You may get a lot more out of it by doing so.

NETWORKING IS GOOD FOR YOU!

The benefits of networking are enormous and must be a part of your career. Don't neglect networking because you feel it's a chore—accept it as a critical part of your position as a health care provider. When you meet people, educate them on who you are, where you are, and what successes you have had doing what you do. Use stories of success to help people understand the value of your work.

Benefits of networking can include:

1. A sense of security in the world around you—you have built a network of resources with people full of special talents. Call upon these talents when you are in need and you will be nurturing your network. This increases your efficiency to solve problems of any size because you will

find that you often know just who to call to fix it when your network is large.

2. New opportunities to build your career. Whether it be a job you are seeking or new clients, building your network will give you "more ears" to listen for you when unique and special opportunities may arise that others could miss simply because the opportunities are not publicized at all. You'll find new ways to give of yourself to others by creating partnerships within your network—potential exposure to ways you can give back are magnified with a large network.

3. Making new friends can be the biggest benefit of all. Sometimes we network simply to create new professional relationships, but over time, you will find that individuals you work with can become friends.

NETWORKING DOES NOT MEAN SELLING

Get it out of your head right now—networking is not selling. I'm not saying you shouldn't bring your appointment book with you because in some circumstances you'll walk away with clients from a networking meeting when you least expected it. But your goal should be to come away from a networking group with another success tally—how many new quality contacts did you make that you will follow up with after the meeting?

Bill Norman and Shelley Johnson-Norman put it very well in their book *The Enviable Lifestyle: Creating a Successful Massage Therapy Business*:

When you network, you converse with people casually and naturally, but you do it with an intention on the long-term potential of building the business relationship. In fact, don't even burden yourself with viewing the business opportunities in attendance. Each person represents a company, a circle of contacts, even if he/she is just a one-employee business. When you talk to a sales rep for a local company, you have to see past her to what she represents. If you spend all your efforts convincing her to get a massage, you miss the chance of developing a relationship where she could introduce you to the entire payroll of employees. Which is better—one massage or a personal introduction to the human resources manager of a 300-employee organization?

NETWORKING NO-NO'S

Being demanding or making others feel obligated to do something for you because you have done something for them is a sure way to destroy a potential referral relationship. When you have done something for someone else, such as send him a referral, be careful not to keep score, much less focus on the score. Keeping score is a bad habit and can make you appear demanding if you make it known what you're doing.

While at a meeting, avoid talking constantly—instead focus on being an effective listener. Networking is about talking to people, training your referral network, and exchanging information. Give your contact enough time to tell you and train you on what it is he or she offers. Don't sequester someone and corner him so he'll listen. Give him some time to hear you and give him the same respect by taking time to hear him. If he has to go, then let him know you'd like to chat with him some more and try to schedule a time for it. If that does not happen, follow up by email or phone to let him know his business is important to you and you want to learn about what it would take to help him build his business. Work to understand him and you will in turn be building a relationship about him understanding you.

In my experience, I have run into people who are fierce about selling their products to me in what should be a casual and friendly networking exchange. Often, these people were folks who wanted me to sell their products for them at my establishment. While I may have trouble with agreeing to sell their kinds of products in my office, many other practitioners would delight in the opportunity to be involved. Since I am extremely active in networking, I am often bombarded by these opportunities to be a distributor, so I have concluded that I won't be a part of a distribution network because of that constant negative bombardment. If I choose a product, it doesn't come with an agreement constantly to push that product or to recruit more people underneath me to do so. I know some people out there have had good experiences with becoming distributors, and I acknowledge that it is a possible new revenue stream for them. However, I caution you to look closely at the bottom line if you are making an ongoing commitment to buy a product and become a distributor. Carrying inventory for these distributors or meeting their quotas can often prove to be problematic for a practitioner on a budget.

> *Story Time:*
>
> *One time, I was at a networking event and stayed a few moments to get to know a member better. As the conversation progressed, I realized this person's only intention was to sell me her product. I felt cornered since I hadn't come to that group to buy something, but to network with other people. After twenty minutes longer than I had planned to spend, I left the meeting feeling like I had just undergone a high-pressure sales situation and loathed the thought of talking to that person again.*
>
> *A short time later, this same person had overheard my scheduling of a one-on-one with another member of the networking group. When the one-on-one happened, she hijacked the meeting and made it completely about herself. The three of us were placed in a very uncomfortable position. This infuriated me, and the whole exchange was tense and sadly didn't go as I had planned. The person I had originally intended to meet with was unhappy with the exchange as well.*

MASTER NETWORKER BEHAVIORS

Gene Hamilton is a master networker and the founder of "I Take the Lead," a smaller and more laid back leads group that focuses on making qualified referrals instead of requiring referrals to be passed in a highly regimented manner. He defined the most successful person in the networking group as:

> They're really more interested in the other person than they are in themselves. They're interested more in giving because they know they'll get; they'll give first and then receive later. They want to make sure that they're helping other people out

and connecting. So it's all about building those relationships rather than just about turning and burning or about selling. Selling is a very "here buy this no okay and here buy this" and they move on. It's about building the relationships and working with people.

Focus your networking energy on being the best networker you can be. According to Donna Fisher, bestselling coauthor of *Power Networking* and *Professional Networking for Dummies*, master networkers display a common set of skills. Those skills are awareness of opportunities, being a helpful person when the occasion arises, honing your communication skills, and practicing a habit of relationship building.

GET THE CONVERSATION GOING

When you meet someone, make small talk to get the ball rolling. Ask open-ended questions and be inclusive of the group if you are speaking in one—listen to the answers and avoid monopolizing the conversation. Avoid controversial or upsetting topics that can take the positive energy right out of the room. Find topics that are appropriate to the situation and focus on them. Ask other people about their outside interests and really get to know each person. Avoid using foul language or commenting on something that could be personal; always speak in a respectful and professional manner—by all means do not gossip. Don't wait for someone else to initiate conversation; simply introduce yourself and ask the other person how he is doing. Every interaction is a new opportunity to create a relationship.

Donna Fisher, author of *Professional Networking for Dummies,* offers the following questions to ask to create constructive small talk:

1. What type of business are you in?

2. How did you get into your work?

3. What do you like most about your work?

4. What advice would you give someone who is entering your line of work?

5. What would you like to be doing in your business that you are not currently doing?

Just as important as being in a conversation is getting out of a conversation gracefully. There are plenty of people out there who don't know when to stop talking. Getting out of a conversation can be one of the hardest skills of all to develop. Sometimes you can spend a lot of time building rapport, but then you want to move on and continue to mingle. There are some situations you just can't get out of gracefully, so say something like, "It was nice to visit with you. I'm going to go over here to do some more mingling. Talk to you again soon!" I often find the most effective technique is to introduce the person to someone else, then tell the two of them about a topic they have in common, and bow out of the conversation gracefully so I can continue to mingle.

LEADS GROUPS

Leads groups are a great way to continue to build solid relationships with others. You meet with the expectation that you are there to learn about other people's businesses and send them business.

In turn, they learn about what you do and send business to you. They become your sales force and you become theirs. Types of leads groups are I Take the Lead, BNI, and LeTip International.

Many different levels of leads groups exist—from rigidly strict to informal and relaxed. Some are very concerned about the time usage in their groups and follow a strictly timed agenda, while others allow time for the conversation to meander or for people to joke. Consider carefully what type of group would be the best fit for your personality type. Are you a person who gets very annoyed when people are late or absent? Then consider a group that penalizes people for being late—perhaps monetarily—because being late or absent is a drain on the group. More laid back groups often have trouble enforcing attendance policies because they may have removed some or all of the restrictions. Poor attendance can create problems with the group's consistency and how seriously people take the functions the group holds. However, highly rigid groups can scare off people who fear that the group time may impede on valuable time at their businesses; for example, if a patient has an emergency and you have no other time to give him, you don't want to be penalized for missing that meeting.

It is wise to visit as many groups as you can before deciding which one is for you. Most of these groups gladly welcome visitors, but they will have a protocol for you to follow. Make sure the prospective group has a spot open for your position before you go; call the group's leader in advance to ask directly. Also, ask the group leader what the agenda will be so you can get an idea of what to expect, such as whether you are even allowed to pass out your business cards.

Misty Nault, MSA, L.Ac., says about her leads group:

> BNI has been a great networking tool for me. It has given me the opportunity to network with a diverse group of people in my community. Many of the people in my group utilize my services and often end up referring their family and friends to me. It accounts for about 40 percent of my client list. It has been useful in other ways as well. As a first time business owner, it has been great to have a network of other business owners I can go to for advice. There is also a network of health care practitioners in the group, which makes for great referral partners, as well as experts in other health-related fields I can go to when I have questions. The other great benefit for me has been getting comfortable talking about what I do. Every week I have to give a commercial for what I can do or what I am looking for. This forces me to be really clear in my mind about what I want my practice to be, and with whom I want to work. The ability to relay this clearly to others is invaluable. I feel confident and at ease when speaking in front of a group of people about what I do. For me, BNI has been great.

Gene Hamilton said about his group "I Take The Lead" (www.ITakeTheLead.com):

> I was in several leads groups, and they went away as groups do. I tried to get into a BNI and I tried to get into a LeTip group, but they just weren't very forthcoming about returning phone calls. Got really frustrated and then I started my own group. It was kind of by accident, but I created it a lot in the image of Toastmasters. You know Toastmasters is a very accepting, inclusive organization. That's what we are

trying to create here. Something that's inexpensive, something that's going to create a true support network—rather than an atmosphere where people beat each other up—and where we support each other because we get beat up in the workplace enough as it is, so I didn't figure people really needed a place where they get beat up again. We're here to support each other; you know, build each other up rather than tear each other down. We want to be here to help each other out.

We're open to everybody, including new people; some groups are like "Well, you're pretty new so why don't you go learn your business and come back." We're here to help people who are just starting out; we want to help people who are stuck in their business; we want to help people who hit a snag in their business, and that's what it's all about because people need a safe environment. So somebody who is new has a place to talk about his business where he's not going to get beat up.

"I Take the Lead" is my personal favorite leads group because of its open laid back style. If you choose to be in "I Take The Lead," tell Gene that Dene sent you.

Many large corporations will require their associates to be part of networking groups. They require it as part of their employees' duties. In rare situations, I have seen smaller clinics ask their employees to be active networkers. Hiring managers often are very impressed by someone who has a networking affiliation on his or her resume. People who have learned and accepted that networking is part of their career as health professionals are the most successful people I have met.

Now you may be saying that all this networking is going to sap you dry of your life force. I have heard this same thing from many health care practitioners. We are often introverted people who work best one-on-one and need to shift our focus from volume to meaningful interactions. Aware of that issue, I ended up starting my own networking group with introverts in mind.

POWER REFERRAL PARTNERS

Consider that a patient may have been in an accident and needs a doctor. That same person may also need a chiropractor, massage therapist, an acupuncturist, a physical therapist, and so on. Knowing the strengths of fellow health care practitioners helps us better to help our patients find the solutions they need more effectively. These types of partnerships can be referred to as Power Referral Partners, and they are often highly sought after in leads groups.

If you're trying to build a practice, it's important to expand your referral base to be as large as you possibly can and to get to know as many other health care practitioners as possible. The reason is not only to be a better practitioner by calling on your resources to help a client/patient, but also so you have the ability to be called upon for your skills as well.

When I first started my practice, Misty and I decided we needed to find a networking group with just health care practitioners, but when I went looking for them, they were few and far between, if not non-existent in some areas. I could find no group that bridged all health care professions in a structured networking environment. That is why the not-for-profit organization Health Care Professionals Referral Networking was created. The group created the opportunity for health care professionals to meet in a free or low-cost structured networking environment designed for introverts. My goal for the group was to meet as many other health care practitioners as possible, which is being achieved by facilitating these networking events for others to do the exact same thing for themselves.

Our group is different than broader purposed networking or lead generation groups. We focus on only health care professionals who have chosen the path of a healer as their career in order to create power referral partnerships. Your profession as a health care provider does not need to be your full-time occupation to join. We recognize that many amazingly talented health care providers start small with little to no advertising budget.

The National Certification Commission for Acupuncture and Oriental Medicine's (NCCAOM) 2008 Job Training Analysis of NCCAOM Diplomats found that 88 percent of respondents to their survey were in solo private practice and that the average annual gross income for all respondents was $41,000-$60,000 per year, and 70.1 percent grossed under $61,000 a year while the average student loan debt was $40,000. In fact, nationwide, as of February 2011, $125,649,795 was the total amount due in student loans for health care related professions with 1,001 borrowers in default.

The statistics clearly show that most practitioners are struggling financially. With these statistics in mind, Health Care Professionals Referral Networking was founded as a "free to join" group with most of our meetings free as well, with the intention of someday becoming a very low cost networking group. We want to help new talent find success and meet other seasoned professionals. Unlike some groups, there are no monetary fines for being late, not referring, or missing meetings. Relationships grow organically in a positive, supportive environment. Our acronym HCPRN is for a reason; PRN means "as needed" in medical terminology. We don't have attendance requirements for our meetings because we know that urgent issues can come up in health care. Our group is meant only to benefit, not to burden its members.

We offer to help build membership in other areas—most organizations do not offer any assistance. Our group is constantly working to expand our reach and if you'd like to help, we would value your willingness to do so. Our members are the key to each other's success, and the growth of the group is the way to their mutual successes.

We understand that for many people, networking is not their gift, so our events are designed to span from what would be great for the shy, one-on-one loving introvert to the amazing open networking extroverts. It is our goal to help teach the skills of networking to our members with our workshops and seminars. Our hope is to be a major source of fundraising for health-related charities with some of the proceeds from these events.

KEY LESSONS:

- Work hard to create "Power Referral Partner" relationships in your networking. Zero in on the potential people who would best complement your work.

- Cross pollinate your networking with leads groups.

Chapter 20

BECOMING A LEADER

Chapter Summary: Become a pillar to your peers by providing a free support group meeting for them to attend—the rewards will be greater than you can imagine. When something is outside of your knowledge and training, don't be afraid to refer to another practitioner. Grow your network to a vast web of people so that the fact that you know a lot of people becomes one of your selling points. When you're ready to cut back on hours in the practice, consider writing a book and becoming a teacher.

GET INVOLVED WITH A PEER SUPPORT GROUP

When I was faced with working for myself for the first time in private practice, I'd say that all the other opportunities I'd ever had to learn about leadership culminated. As I ran my own business for the first time, the ideas vanished that I could rely on a steady paycheck from someone else, and I started to learn what it meant to be "on your own." There was no support group in the area where I could bounce questions off people who were willing to listen. I felt I had no choice but to go it alone.

While I would later have some incredible opportunities to be a leader, that first year of being on my own straight out of school is what really shaped my opinions. I knew in my heart there needed to be better support networks for people like me, and I decided that once I had the experience to create it, I would.

One day later in my career, I was working with a more senior therapist. She was the type who liked to tell you what to do because she knew what to do—all the time. When I was momentarily struggling with an oddly behaved client, she told me to join a support group to discuss my thoughts and feelings. I thought that was a fantastic idea, so I asked her where I could find one. She couldn't seem to tell me.

Over the years in my career, I've had various opportunities to be an examiner or a guest speaker at schools. It's been a joy for me to have these opportunities, and I soon found out from these experiences that many other people wanted a group; they just did not feel that the commitment to create one was something they were willing to undertake.

In reality, the support group itself took less than ten hours a month of my time to create, promote, attend, and manage, with about four meetings in different areas a month. But the satisfaction from helping others to achieve successful careers and promote the longevity of their careers was something I had never realized would impact me as much as it did. I started the group upon the premise that I didn't know everything, but if I and the other members put our heads together, we could figure out almost anything or find the right people to ask for answers. Making your mark on your profession by being there for others is one of the most satisfying feelings I have ever experienced. If that feeling is what it means to be a leader, I only wish I had started sooner.

In my experience, it is difficult to collect a fee for a support group, so try not to consider it as a new source of revenue, but instead as a way to serve your profession. I have seen other groups have trouble by trying to collect fees. A group must provide a lot of value to collect fees, and free continuing education credits aren't always enough to incite attendance at meetings. Most of your meetings need to be free to get interest going first before you start to charge. People need to know what they are paying for, and if they aren't getting enough out of the meetings to warrant the cost of their time, they won't want to pay.

Our format for our support meetings is simple. We use the events website Meetup.com to organize ourselves. We get together once a month in a given area at a coffee house or a breakfast restaurant. We limit the group to a maximum of ten attendees to keep it personal and small. Our agenda features our announcements, upcoming meetings, and suggested introduction for members so they can articulate who they are to the group and what they need to get out of the group meeting that day.

DEFER TO OTHERS' EXPERTISE

Networking with others in your profession is helpful for so many reasons, but learning to call upon their strengths and be a people "connector" will open up many more doors. When you begin your odyssey of being a health care practitioner, it is your duty to become the best possible resource you can for your patients. You need to know how to solve problems, and if you don't know how to solve them, you need to know who can. Stay in the scope of your practice and follow your instincts about giving a referral to someone who may have more knowledge in any given area.

For example, I have worked with many other practitioners and wellness product salespeople who claim to have a vast knowledge of nutrition. While I cannot speak for what training these people have had, at no time during my training as a massage therapy practitioner did I learn about nutrition; therefore, I consider it outside of the scope of my practice to provide advice on this topic. Some people may sneer at this perceived shortcoming, but the truth is that I would rather not carry a partner product I cannot fully explain to my patients. I take this opportunity to refer people to a nutritionist I trust who has much more background and training in the area. Nutrition is a complicated subject, and I cannot justify selling a product in my office when I truly do not have a deep understanding of how it works. I would look like a fool if my clients asked me about the product since I would have no idea how to answer them in scientific detail even if a vendor had given me a "thorough training." Even with all the training that many nutrition product systems provide, that training will never equate to what a nutritionist has to learn in a formalized degree program.

Referring to another person's expertise is not showing a weakness in your own expertise—it's showing that you know other people who have the expertise sought after and it proves that having a big network is very powerful. You cannot be all things to all people, and you cannot have all the answers to all the questions all the time. It just doesn't work. In *Four Disciplines of Execution*, Stephen Covey states that humans are wired to do only one thing right at a time. Consider this in your own practice as a tip not to try to do everything, but call on your network to help you fill in the gaps in your skills. These gaps are not weaknesses—they are opportunities to build a referral relationship with another practitioner. We are all good at our own niches, and it is your duty as a health care practitioner to know the strengths of others around you.

Quite a few patients of mine tell me they wish their doctor had known about the capabilities of massage to treat certain conditions and suggested it to them earlier in their treatment process. The only way we can make this kind of request happen is by networking all professions across each other in an effort to learn about new techniques so we can properly care for our patients.

When Misty and I and the other early members of Health Care Professionals Referral Networking grew the organization, we did it upon the premise that we needed to learn as much as we could about as many other health practitioners, no matter their approaches, to create strong referral relationships, and promote the advancement of integrative medicine. In our meetings, we would take time to introduce ourselves, let everyone know where we were located, and recall a recent success story. This group grew quickly and is fostering an atmosphere of helpfulness, creating what I like to call a "living bridge" between professions. We work hard to change the mindset of viewing folks in the same profession as competition. We all have our strengths, and we call upon each other to help fill in our weaknesses. We may treat the same ailment or body part as someone else, but it is important to know about that other professional's approach just in case you have that one patient who needs a different approach.

I respect the members of HCPRN; they are leaders for working to create a new efficiency in medicine by helping their patients find solutions to their problems faster through knowing what other treatment methods are available. The members have taken the initiative to join such a group in order to improve their abilities to call upon others.

Imagine if you have a patient who is leaving the area and asks you where he can find someone like you in the area where he is moving. That question is one of the hardest to answer because it is very difficult to know everyone everywhere. I once had a patient in Chicago call me about my services doing intra-oral massage because she was hoping I would know someone in her area who provided the same services. Her dentist had recommended this approach, so she had gone online to research it and found me via my website articles. In this particular case, the state of Illinois has different laws with which I wasn't familiar and there is no professional association for people who use this technique. While I was unable to find a contact for her in her area, by calling upon a network, many of us would be able to help our patients in this way to find reliable providers close to where they live.

Do your best also to attend conventions, workshops, and networking groups in other areas whenever possible. Granted, it is much more difficult to attend the further away you are, but it can pay off when you know someone extremely special who can help that one client you have who cannot find a solution any other way. You don't have to be the provider of the solution every time—you will become the hero of the day just by knowing where to find the solution. Be your patient's personal Yellow Pages and reap the amazing rewards of being a connector.

> *Story Time:*
>
> *One massage therapist I know refuses to attend any networking meetings or massage therapy events. Unfortunately, she is doing herself a great disservice by waiting for patients to be handed to her by her employer and considering her position just a job. The problem she has created is that she has no network of people to call upon for support should she encounter any trouble along the way, no resources to check with when her patients have problems she can't solve, and most likely, a shorter career because of the disconnection from the community to which she really belongs. This therapist will likely never become a leader because only a few even know she exists. In respect to introverts, I know it's hard to put yourself out there, but it is so essential to do so in our profession.*

BECOME A MENTOR

One of the best things about being a mentor is that it's not being a manager. You're not looking to be responsible for someone's success—you are his or her trusted advisor only. One of the fastest ways to become someone people look up to for advice is to make yourself available to students. Simply being a speaker at a school makes you a resource for the institution and its students. Contact your instructors and tell them you are available to be a speaker or serve on a panel for their classes. I have had many opportunities simply because I reach out to instructors to tell them I am available.

Attending the support meetings made it incredibly easy to find a way to mentor others. I shouldered the burden of being a mentor with other senior therapists at the group. It was a great way to pool our collective knowledge so we were a resource to people who were new to the profession. We were there to comfort them when times were tough and to offer new fresh perspectives when they needed it. We bounced opinions around and weighed pros and cons. It became my conclusion then that this method was by far the simplest way to become a mentor to others.

BECOME AN EXPERT

A business tactic that will provide results you can't even comprehend is becoming a published expert on a given topic. When I was writing this book, I experienced a peculiar phenomenon. I noticed that I had far less people sitting by me in networking meetings before I mentioned I was working on a book than after I announced it. The difference was night and day. People nearly always sit by me at networking meetings now, whereas before there always seemed to be at least one empty chair between us. Perhaps it was simply because I had something they possibly would need, such as having their comments published in my book so they could be considered as experts.

Becoming perceived as an expert is not as difficult as you might imagine. Judge Huss and Marlene Coleman note in their book *Start Your Own Medical Practice: A Guide to All the Things They Don't Teach You in Medical School about Starting Your Own Practice*: "Acting as a speaker for civic organizations is a very good way of making yourself known as a doctor and an expert in your field."

Help a Reporter Out (HARO—www.HelpaReporter.com) is a plethora of opportunities for free publicity for experts just waiting to happen. Sign up at the site if you'd like to be potentially interviewed by a reporter, an author, or columnist from all kinds of different publications. You may land a dream media opportunity.

Another incredible way to build your reputation in a community is to be available for speaking engagements. If you don't feel comfortable speaking in front of a group, consider joining a local Toastmasters (www.toastmasters.org) to network and learn more about speaking in front of a group. Participating in this organization is a great way to get over your fears. When you're ready to speak, visit Speaker Match (www.speakermatch.com) and sign yourself up as an expert to talk on your specialty. If you plan well and put an earnest effort behind this strategy, it will open so many new doors for you.

WRITE A BOOK, BECOME A TEACHER

One of the projects I worked on during my consulting career was a strategy plan for the sales curriculum at Microsoft. It was a huge project to gather the requirements for the curriculum by asking each manager, across what was actually only a fraction of this gigantic organization, what was a priority for their sales teams. We focused on what would make ideal salespeople and pieced together their training plans based on the courses they needed for the competencies that were considered to be the building blocks of the most successful people in the organization. I was fascinated by the intricacies the managers considered for training their teams. They truly were doing it because they wanted their employees to be the best they could possibly be, not solely for the company's bottom line, but also for the employees' personal growth.

I believe teachers are among the most respected people because the best ones care deeply about their students' successes and work hard to teach them something of value. Take a moment to reminiscence about your experiences in school. Who made the biggest impact on you? Chances are it was your favorite teachers. When I think of amazing teachers, I remember the vivid pictures my English teacher, Professor Cathy McDonald, made while she was teaching. A dynamic speaker, she brought stories to life in ways I can only dream of doing. Her style and flair is something I measure myself against when I speak to a group. Her methods were so effective that I can still clearly remember watching her teach the class to this day. She gave me my love of writing by making it so interesting that it became my favorite subject in school.

One of the most inspirational people in my career is my first term massage teacher, Janis Lynne, LMP. She was the first person who really showed me what it looked like to be a massage therapist who had been in her career for over twenty years. She taught some of the most memorable classes I had in massage school. To this day, I think many other students formed a bond with her just like I did because she demonstrates so well what it means to be a mentor in our field.

Shortly after a back injury doing my work, I had one of my late evening calls with Janis to catch up. When I told her about how I had just hurt my back from working, she told me, "Dene, you need to cut back on your hours, write a book, and teach a class, but I bet you'll just take too long to do it." Anybody who knows me realizes that making a statement like that is like a triple dog dare to me.

Those words were all it took for me to go hire a publishing coach, Patrick Snow, to help coach me to write this book. Then I hired Shuna Morelli, LMP, to consult me on how to create a workshop. I wrote and published this book and composed my first workshop in fifty-six days just so I could send Janis a signed copy of my book and the continuing education calendar with my class on it. I may have lost a bunch of sleep in the process of writing this book because of the ridiculous deadline I set for myself, but the long-lasting effects of her mentoring are going to show in my increased longevity and career satisfaction.

It's a gift to be an excellent teacher. Moving into this stage of your career will most likely be an extremely smart move if you've been in the work you're doing for a long time or would like to continue your work with a lesser number of patients per week. I chose to make these changes because my body told me it wanted part-time hands-on work, I listened to my mentor's 20/20 hindsight, and I followed the passion for writing that a fantastic teacher inspired within me. I give credit to Professor Cathy McDonald's amazing English classes and my mentoring from Janis Lynne, LMP, for why this book was written.

If you want to write a book and teach a class, give Patrick and Shuna a call and tell them Dene sent you.

Patrick Snow -
www.PatrickSnow.com

Shuna Morelli, LMP -
www.SouthSoundMassageEducation.com

KEY LESSONS:

- Start a peer support group in your area if there isn't one already.

- If there is a support group nearby, participate and volunteer to help!

- Don't charge for a support group—it's going to be uphill to get people to go when they are really down and out.

- If you don't know something, don't be afraid to send the patient to someone who does.

- Provide service to the community and become a pillar of the community.

- Mentoring is an easy way to start a path to leadership.

- When the time comes, cut back on practice hours, write a book, and go teach.

BIBLIOGRAPHY

Ancowitz, Nancy. *Self-Promotion for Introverts: The Quiet Guide to Getting Ahead.* New York, NY: McGraw Hill.

Baker, Wayne. *Achieving Success Through Social Capital.* San Francisco, CA: Jossey-Bass.

Blanchard, Ken. *The Referral of a Lifetime: The Networking System That Produces Bottom Line Results Every Day.* San Francisco, CA: Barrett-Koehler Publishers.

Blanchard, Kenneth and Spencer Johnson. *The One Minute Manager.* New York, NY: William Morrow.

Buford, MD, FACS, Gregory A. and Steven E. House. *Beauty and the Business: Practice, Profits, and Productivity, Performance and Profitability.* Garden City, NY: Morgan James Publishing.

Canfield, Jack and Janet Switzer. *The Success Principles: How to Get from Where You Are to Where You Want to Be.* New York, NY: William Morrow.

Covey, Stephen. *Four Disciplines of Execution.* Salt Lake City, UT: Covey.

Covey, Stephen. *Seven Habits of Highly Effective People.* Salt Lake City, UT: Covey.

Ellis, Keith. *The Magic Lamp: Goal Setting for People Who Hate Setting Goals.* New York, NY: Three Rivers Press.

Fisher, Donna. *Professional Networking for Dummies.* New York, NY: Hungry Minds.

Fisher, Donna and Sandy Vilas. *Power Networking.* Austin, TX: Bard Press.

Gage, David. *The Partnership Charter: How to Start Out Right.* New York, NY: Basic Books.

Hill, Napoleon. *Think and Grow Rich.* Plainview, NY: Tribeca Books.

Hill, Napoleon and W. Stone. *Success Through a Positive Mental Attitude.* New York, NY: Simon & Schuster.

Holub, LMT, Megan. *How to Make $100,000 per year as a Massage Therapist.* Seattle, WA: Olive Vine Press.

Huss, Judge and Marlene Coleman. *Start Your Own Medical Practice: A Guide to All the Things They Don't Teach You In Medical School about Starting Your Own Practice.* Naperville, IL: Sphinx Publishing.

Johnson, Spencer. *Peaks and Valleys: Making Good and Bad Times Work for You—At Work and In Life.* New York, NY: Atria Books.

Kroeger, Otto and Janet Thuesen. *Type Talk.* New York, NY: Dell Publishing.

Lemay, Eunice and Jane Schwamberger. *Listen Up!: How to Communicate Effectively at Work*. Santa Cruz, CA: Papilio Publishing.

Lesser, Eric. *Knowledge and Social Capital*. New York, NY: Butterworth-Heinemann.

Maxwell, John C. *Mentoring 101*. Nashville, TN: Thomas Nelson.

Maxwell, John C. *Relationships 101*. Nashville, TN: Thomas Nelson.

Maxwell, John C. *The 21 Irrefutable Laws of Leadership: Follow Them and People Will Follow You*. Nashville, TN: Thomas Nelson.

Misner, Ivan, David Alexander, and Brian Hilliard. *Networking Like a Pro: Turning Contacts into Connections*. Irvine, CA: Entrepreneur Press.

Morgenstern, Julie. *Time Management from the Inside Out, Second Edition: The Foolproof System for Taking Control of Your Schedule—and Your Life*. New York, NY: Holt Paperbacks.

Morris, Rick A. and Brette McWhorter Sember. *Project Management That Works: Real-World Advice on Communicating, Problem-Solving, and Everything Else You Need to Know to Get the Job Done*. AMACOM.

Norman, Bill and Shelley Johnson-Norman. *The Enviable Lifestyle: Creating a Successful Massage Therapy Business*. Charleston, SC: BookSurge Publishing.

Olsen, Larry. *Get a Vision and Live It: Becoming Prosperous Now for Life.* Harrison, NY: Book Clearing House.

Pond, Jonathan. *Safe Money in Tough Times: Everything You Need to Know to Survive the Financial Crisis.* Columbus, OH: McGraw-Hill.

Ryback, David, Jill Cathcart, and David Nour. *ConnectAbility: 8 Keys to Building Stronger Partnerships with Your Colleagues and Your Customers.* Columbus, OH: McGraw-Hill.

Snow, Patrick. *Creating Your Own Destiny.* Hoboken, NJ: John Wiley & Sons.

Snow, Patrick. *The Affluent Entrepreneur: 20 Proven Principles for Achieving Prosperity.* Hoboken, NJ: John Wiley & Sons.

Stanley, Kay B. and Jeffery Daigrepont. *Starting a Medical Practice: The Physician's Handbook for Successful Practice Start-Up.* Chicago, IL: American Medical Association.

Stoddard, David A. and Robert J. Tamasy. *Ten Proven Principles for Developing People to Their Fullest Potential.* Colorado Springs, CO: NavPress.

Stoltz, Paul G. *Adversity Quotient: Turning Obstacles into Opportunities.* Hoboken, NJ: John Wiley & Sons.

Stoltzfus, Tony. *Coaching Questions: A Coach's Guide to Powerful Asking Skills.* Virginia Beach, VA: Pegasus Creative Arts.

Tamm, James W. and Ronald J. Luyet. *Radical Collaboration: Five Essential Skills to Overcome Defensiveness and Build Successful Relationships.* New York, NY: Harper Paperbacks.

Wildermuth, Anna. *Change One Thing: Discover What's Holding You Back—and Fix It—With the Secrets of a Top Executive Image Consultant.* Columbus, OH: McGraw-Hill.

Wooden, John. *They Call Me Coach.* Columbus, OH: McGraw-Hill.

Young, Linda. "Not so fast my online advertising friend: Online advertising—Taking a long term view." *Advertising and Marketing Review* (April 2010).

Zachary, Lois J. *The Mentor's Guide: Facilitating Effective Learning Relationships.* New York, NY: Jossey-Bass Books.

Zack, Devora. *Networking for People Who Hate Networking: A Field Guild for Introverts, the Overwhelmed, and the Underconnected.* San Francisco, CA: Barrett-Koehler Publishers.

BUILDING AN AMAZING CAREER CHALLENGE

While writing this book, I dealt with a great deal of angst hoping that I fully addressed every little thing I should have known when I started out in my career. Handing off this first edition to the editor was excruciating since I just wanted to put more and more information in it. In this first edition, I interviewed people in health professions all over the country, seeking those people who may have some insight. With due diligence, I did all I could to keep their stories in this book whether they wished to contribute anonymously or share their identity. I am fully aware though that there are probably still some valuable things I have left out or have yet to learn about myself.

If you feel I completely left out something that is vitally important to this book, I challenge you to write to me about it and share a story from which everyone can learn. The story will be considered for the next edition of this book.

Visit our website at www.BuildinganAmazingCareer.com and tell me what you think we should include in the next edition of this book. Save someone else hours of agony learning a hard lesson, have the satisfaction of knowing you made an impact on the future success of other health care professionals, and get some free PR for your practice.

BUILDING AMAZING PARTNERSHIPS CHALLENGE

Misty Nault, MSA, L.Ac. and I are working on the second book in the Building an Amazing Career series. We would like to hear your stories about successful health care partnerships between individuals. Long after the first book is published, we will still accept submissions for new editions.

This book is specifically about how to build profitable referral partnerships and marketing partnerships for health care professionals. The type of content we want to see is from submissions by email only—if we like your submission, we may contact you for a phone interview or we may take your submission as your wrote it.

Submissions from marketing firms are considered secondary. We are looking to feature health professionals from around the U.S.

The type of things we are looking for are:

1. Medical Doctors in group settings co-marketing their group together at large group practices or hospitals

    a. How they accomplished an amazing campaign

b. Any details of the campaign strategy execution

   c. Budgets of their large campaigns (estimates are fine)

2. How small medical practices became large

   a. History behind the transition from small to big

   b. Hardships encountered and how they were dealt with

   c. Turnover thoughts on keeping teams

   d. Marketing campaigns that were the ones that "did it" best

3. Partnerships and Legalities

   a. How did your group practice organize itself legally with contracts (examples of contracts would be appreciated greatly)?

   b. What was your experience with hiring lawyers to help with the process?

   c. What legalities did you consider when creating your partnership?

4. How sole practitioners partnered with other sole practitioners

   a. How was the initial partnership trust established?

   b. What was the marketing activity?

   c. What was the key to making this relationship successful?

d. Any details on budgets

5. Low budget marketing

   a. What was your best low budget campaign?

   b. How did you build word-of-mouth for your medical practice?

   c. What were your experiences with advertising?

You can answer any or all of the questions in depth. Visit our website at www.hcprn.org to tell us what you think we should include in this book, share your stories, and get some free PR for your practice.

ABOUT
HEALTH CARE PROFESSIONALS REFERRAL NETWORKING

Health Care Professionals Referral Networking (HCPRN), a not-for-profit organization, seeks to promote integrative medicine and raise funds for medical research. We work hard to empower health care professionals to dissolve our view of each other as competitors and to change our mindsets to be collaborators strengthening one another's mutual opportunities for success. Our group facilitates teaching each other about our healing gifts and learning what works for our patients. We use a part of the proceeds from our events to fund medical research to promote our desire to be ever more ready for our clients and patients' needs.

Our group was founded in Seattle, Washington in February 2011, and it is growing every day with other health care professionals who are looking to learn all they can about other treatment techniques and build solid referral relationships with other health care providers of all kinds.

If you would like to have an HCPRN chapter in your city, inquire for more information. Call (888) 823-7381 or visit www.hcprn.org

ABOUT NORTHWEST LMP SUPPORT GROUP

Our group was born with the idea that there are simply not enough local ways for bodyworkers and massage therapists to meet in a safe environment to talk about their work with other bodyworkers in a non-competitive, non-judgmental atmosphere.

This group is intended to create a safe space for LMP's to network, discuss work, discuss issues, share treatment ideas, talk about injuries, and support each other. Any currently Licensed Massage Practitioner who is practicing or injured is welcome to join us. Our group is free to join and most of the meetings are free.

It is our mission to help raise money for the Massage Therapy Foundation while creating a way to keep massage therapists satisfied and in their careers longer. We provide study groups to new practitioners prepping for their board exams to help foster them into the profession in a supportive way. We recruit teachers to come in and give demonstrations of techniques that would be valuable for the group members to learn.

We are looking to add groups in the Washington, Oregon, and Idaho region to our group site to give new leaders an opportunity to call upon the network and tools we have already built upon. If you would like to start a group in one of these areas, please contact us.

Visit our site at: www.hcprn.org and select the link for NW LMP Support Group.

ABOUT THE AUTHOR

Jodene "Dene" Hager, LMP realized from a young age that she wasn't a fan of big crowds, but she found a need to help others. She knew her lack of confidence in approaching others and talking in large groups would stop her growth, so she set out to change herself through hard work and learning about others who were successful in overcoming their fears.

> *Do what you fear and fear disappears.*
> — David Joseph Schwartz

She stepped outside her comfort zone again and again to learn something new about expanding her heart out to others. During a time in her varied career, she coordinated trade shows, she learned how salespeople put themselves out there to strangers, she learned how to be approachable and how to approach a stranger. Working full-time during the day, she attended massage school night classes full-time to follow her passion for hands-on bodywork. Upon graduation, she started her own business and eventually managed the massage practice for two clinics leading them to an all time high in their success.

Dene had her passion stripped from her by a terrible injury received from doing the work itself. It was through this experience that she learned about the value of work-life balance and self-care. This injury caused her to return to the corporate world and learn yet even more about people, business, and the pursuit of success. In this reluctant transition, she experienced even more adventures in consulting, and she learned the things corporate America has learned, but the world of health care is far behind in learning. In the corporate world, she was a business consultant sent to such companies at T-Mobile, Microsoft, BP, and Intel as a project manager or business analyst. She learned about what it took to be a consultant, and she learned how much not following your passion can take from your soul.

When the economic downturn hit, Dene once again found herself looking for a means to an income. It was time to go back to bodywork since her body had healed in the time away. She embraced coming back to the work she loved and jumped in heart first. She took part-time jobs as an employee to get back into the work. In a short while, she was offered a position at Group Health Research Institute where she learned about medical research. After her commitment concluded, she became a full-time self-employed therapist in a partnership with Misty Nault, MSA, L.Ac. at NW Pain Relief.

This book marks the beginning of sharing the lessons she has learned along the way by being an entrepreneur, an employee, and an independent contractor in massage therapy while working with a wide variety of other health professionals in different settings.

ATTEND A SEMINAR BY DENE

When it comes to knowing how to share our gifts, most of us don't even know how to articulate them. We don't know if we're legitimate, and we question ourselves over and over again more than anyone else might.

Dene has created a way to energize and inspire health care practitioners to "come out of the closet" with their gifts and share them with the world through her course series "Share Your Gifts." This interactive, experiential learning class gets people up out of their seats and teaches them how to drum up business in ways not previously taught before in a business class for health care practitioners.

Dene's teaching strategy is entertaining and full of techniques to ignite passion in her students to help them walk away with a new way to achieve lasting success in their careers. The techniques don't just apply to Dene's passion of massage therapy, but to all health care providers looking to share their gifts with the world.

Contact Dene by phone to learn more about booking her to speak at your school or event at (888) 823-7381 or email Dene at Dene@NWPainRelief.com. To see a highlight video, visit the Health Care Professionals Referral Networking website: www.hcprn.org

VISIT OUR WEBSITE

Visit **www.hcprn.org** to read more about our networking group, get valuable resources and tips for your practice, find out about books you should read, and learn about opportunities to network.

NO GROUP NEARBY?

We are looking for people who are leaders and who want to become chapter organizers for Health Care Professionals Referral Networking anywhere people feel there is a need. Please visit our website at www.hcprn.org to contact us for more information.

GET QUANTITY DISCOUNTS

Building an Amazing Career is available at quantity discounts for orders of ten or more copies. Please see www.hcprn.org for more information.